BREAKING GROUND

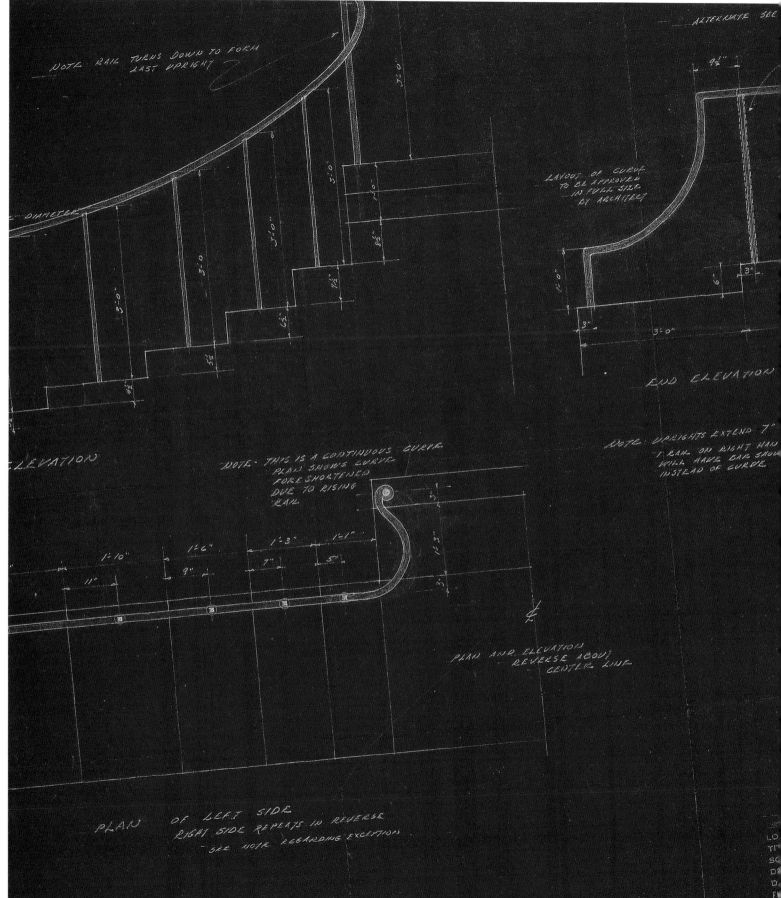

NOTE RAIL TURNS DOWN TO FORM LAST UPRIGHT

DIAMETER

LAYOUT OF CURVE TO BE APPROVED IN FULL SIZE BY ARCHITECT

ALTERNATE SEE

END ELEVATION

NOTE: UPRIGHTS EXTEND 7"
RAIL ON RIGHT HAND
WILL HAVE BAR SHOU
INSTEAD OF CURVE

ELEVATION

NOTE- THIS IS A CONTINUOUS CURVE
PLAN SHOWS CURVE
FORESHORTENED
DUE TO RISING
RAIL

PLAN AND ELEVATION
REVERSE ABOUT
CENTER LINE

PLAN OF LEFT SIDE
RIGHT SIDE REPEATS IN REVERSE
- SEE NOTE REGARDING EXCEPTION

WITH APPRECIATION FOR THE SUPPORT OF THESE ORGANIZATIONS

FRIENDS OF MODERN ARCHITECTURE/LINCOLN [MA]

Founded 2005

The Friends of Modern Architecture/Lincoln (FoMA) was formed to promote wider knowledge and appreciation of modern houses and their benefits, and to help in efforts to preserve them for future generations of homeowners. FoMA is dedicated to building awareness of Lincoln's exceptional stock of early modern houses, acknowledging these as an important component of Lincoln's historical and cultural heritage.

LINCOLN HISTORICAL SOCIETY [MA]

Founded 1961

The Lincoln Historical Society was founded to preserve the town's rich history, and to educate the public about this history, with the goal of fostering civic participation by members of the Lincoln community. Through public programs, exhibits, commemorative plaques, book publishing, and special projects, the Society undertakes to preserve the town's historical treasures, and to increase awareness of its political, social, and cultural heritage.

HENRY B. HOOVER

NEW ENGLAND MODERN ARCHITECT

BREAKING

LUCRETIA HOOVER GIESE AND HENRY B. HOOVER JR.

Friends of Modern Architecture / Lincoln (FoMA / Lincoln)

In Association with University Press of New England, Hanover and London

GROUND

Friends of Modern Architecture/Lincoln (FoMA/Lincoln)

In Association with University Press of New England

www.upne.com

© 2015 Henry B. Hoover Jr. and Lucretia Hoover Giese

Manufactured in China

Designed and typeset in Albertina by Mindy Basinger Hill

For permission to reproduce any of the material

in this book, contact Permissions, University Press

of New England, One Court Street, Suite 250,

Lebanon NH 03766; or visit www.upne.com

Library of Congress Cataloging-in-Publication Data

Giese, Lucretia H.

Breaking ground: Henry B. Hoover, New England

modern architect / Lucretia Hoover Giese and

Henry B. Hoover Jr.

      pages   cm

Includes bibliographical references and index.

ISBN 978-0-692-29715-5 (pbk.: alk. paper)

1. Hoover, Henry B.—Criticism and interpretation.

2. Modern movement (Architecture)—New England.

I. Hoover, Henry B., Jr. II. Title.

NA737.H615G54 2015

720.92—dc23   2014041231

5   4   3   2   1

DEDICATED TO HENRY BROWN AND LUCRETIA JONES HOOVER,
AND TO ELIZABETH HOOVER NORMAN AND PAUL ERNST GIESE

CONTENTS

List of Illustrations x

Foreword xiii

Acknowledgments xvii

Introduction xix

1 Education 1

2 Fletcher Steele Years 12

3 First Houses 18

4 War Years 33

5 Postwar Houses 36

6 The Prolific Decade 46

7 Hoover and Hill Associates 78

8 Industrial Design 81

9 Late Work 89

10 Final Word 99

Afterword 101

Appendix A: Chronology 103

Appendix B: Lincoln Public Library Project 105

Appendix C: Architectural Projects 109

Notes 117

Index 139

ILLUSTRATIONS

Historic New England Archives has accepted the future donation of the HBH Papers, including architectural plans and drawings, and selected furnishings of the Hoover House.

I.1. Henry B. Hoover on site, ca. 1957   xx

1.1. The Pantheon, Rome, Hoover student drawing, ca. 1920–23   2

1.2. "Pantheon, Rome." The University Prints   3

1.3. "A Flagstaff Base," Hoover competition drawing, ca. 1923–24   5

1.4. Thesis Design, Hoover drawing, 1924   5

1.5. Letter from Fletcher Steele to "Hoover," dated May 10, 1925   9

1.6. Bernini's St. Peter's Piazza, Hoover Fellowship drawing, ca. 1927   10

2.1. "The Perugino View," Naumkeag, Hoover drawing for Fletcher Steele, 1931   13

2.2. Memorial for Mrs. John Forbes, Hoover drawing, 1932   15

2.3. "Plan of Left Side" of the Blue Steps, Naumkeag, Hoover drawing, dated September 13, 1938   16

2.4. Blue Steps, Naumkeag   17

3.1. "View from Living Court." Hoover drawing, 1935   19

3.2. Landscape plan by Hoover for Hoover House   20

3.3. "North Elevation, South Elevation." Hoover drawing, ca. 1937   21

3.4. South elevation, 1937 Hoover House   22

3.5. Cambridge Reservoir from 1937 Hoover House   23

3.6. Plan of 1937 Hoover House   24

3.7. Interior showing Hoover-designed marble-top table, ca. 1937   25

3.8. Plan of 1955 Hoover House   26

3.9. South elevation, 1955 Hoover House   27

3.10. Plan of Gilboy House   28

3.11. North elevation, Gilboy House   29

3.12. South elevation, Gilboy House   30

3.13. Interior of Gilboy House with Hoover-designed furniture   31

4.1. Hoover working with student   34

5.1. West elevation, DeNormandie House   37

5.2. Plan of DeNormandie House   38

5.3. Plan of Fitts House   39

5.4. West elevation, Fitts House   40

5.5. Living room, Fitts House   41

5.6. Original cabinetry separating dining room and kitchen, Fitts House   41

5.7. West elevation, former Pierce-Ropes House   42

5.8. Plan of Heck House   44

5.9. West elevation, Heck House   45

6.1. Plan for Wilkoff House   47

6.2. West elevation, Adler House   48

6.3. Plan of Adler House   49

6.4. South elevation, Adler House   50

6.5. View of Cambridge Reservoir from Adler House   51

6.6. South elevation, Moor House   52

6.7. Terrace, Moor House 53

6.8. Pavilion, Moor House 54

6.9. Plan of Peavy House 55

6.10. Northwest elevation, Peavy House 56

6.11. Southeast elevation, Peavy House 56

6.12. Southeast elevation with master bedroom wing, Peavy House 57

6.13. South elevation, Satterfield House 59

6.14. Living room, Satterfield House 59

6.15. Plan of Satterfield House 60

6.16. Plan of Schmertzler-Osborne House 61

6.17. Living/dining area, Schmertzler-Osborne House 62

6.18. North elevation, Schmertzler-Osborne House 62

6.19. Receipt detailing construction expenses 63

6.20. Plan of Germeshausen House 64

6.21. West elevation, Germeshausen House 65

6.22. Interior of Germeshausen House 65

6.23. View from west elevation through interior of Germeshausen House 66

6.24. Southeast elevation, Shearer House 68

6.25. Southwest elevation, Shearer House 69

6.26. Plan of Shearer House 70

6.27. Staircase in entry hall, Shearer House 71

6.28. Living room with view of dining area, Shearer House 72

6.29. Living room, Shearer House 73

6.30. View of Mt. Monadnock from dining room, Shearer House 73

6.31. South elevation, Maclaurin House 74

6.32. East elevation, Maclaurin House 74

6.33. Plan of Maclaurin House 75

6.34. Entry hall, Maclaurin House 76

8.1. "One large machine" drawing 82

8.2. "Bowling pin sorter" drawing 83

8.3. "R2D2" drawing 85

8.4. *Buy Yourself* brochure: "Recorder" and "Auto-Collector Cabinets" 86

8.5. *Buy Yourself* brochure: Procedure 86

8.6. *Buy Yourself* brochure: Marketing 86

8.7. *Buy Yourself* brochure: Cover 87

9.1. South elevation, Wade House 88

9.2. Plan of Wade House 90

9.3. Aerial view of Ritsher House 92

9.4. Plan of Ritsher House 93

9.5. South elevation, Ritsher House 94

9.6. West elevation, Giese House 95

9.7. Plan of Giese House 96

9.8. Causeway, Satterfield House 97

10.1. Hoover in living room of 1937 Hoover House 98

B.1. South elevation, Lincoln Public Library 106

B.2. Plan of Lincoln Public Library addition 106

FOREWORD

It is often said that modern architecture is an acquired taste, but what is less stated is the power that this acquisition can have in shaping one's future. At the age of thirteen, I visited friends who had recently moved from an eighteenth-century farmhouse into one of The Architects Collaborative (TAC)–designed houses at Six Moon Hill in Lexington, Massachusetts. My reaction upon walking into this house was immediate and transformative—this was architecture that could speak to the spirit and the heart—and could do so with incredible economy of means. Why even consider any other way to live, or in my case, for that matter, consider becoming anything except an architect? I had a similar experience twenty-five years later when, after a year of house hunting, my wife and I first walked into what was advertised as a modest "contemporary" along a scenic road in Weston. Although smaller than almost any other house we had seen in our long search, the space inside was a revelation—open, gracious, simply but beautifully detailed and so well connected to its site that it felt like a natural feature of the wooded landscape. Within five minutes we knew we were home.

The architect of the house was Henry B. Hoover, who, though I never met him, has subsequently had an outsized influence upon both my personal life and my professional trajectory as an architect. One of my biggest surprises in finding this house was simply that I had never heard of Henry Hoover; this to me and many like-minded colleagues bespoke a significant gap in the record of the evolution of the modern domestic landscape, and it is extremely gratifying, after more than two decades of advocacy in behalf of Hoover and other pioneering New England modernists, to be given the privilege to contribute to this work, which should go a long way to establishing the importance of Hoover's contribution to the illustrious history of modernism in this region.

The Metro-west Boston suburbs are home to some of the most important modern houses and modern house developments in the United States, a logical extension (or bedroom community, if you like) of the mind-set and patronage that made Boston and Cambridge the locus of a collection of institutional and public works of modernism that are rarely equaled and never exceeded anywhere in the United States. Although Lexington and Concord have more houses, Lincoln's inventory is arguably the most diverse and architecturally significant—and modernism began in Lincoln with Henry Hoover.

The modern movement in New England—like New England itself—was built upon ideas and traditions that were always strongly informed by outsiders like Hoover; this is a phenomenon that began with the Puritans and continues to this day. Those that made the decision to settle in New England first generated and subsequently built upon the particular intellectual fortitude and creative energy necessary to thrive in the physical and cultural landscape of this region. By the 1930s there was no doubt that modernity—as a function of philosophy, science, social justice, and economy—was an established and largely welcome presence among the progressive minds of New England, many of whom, like Henry Hoover, were now prepared to accept modernism in the arts as well.

Hoover was part of a rarified group of first-generation modernists, trained in the Beaux-Arts or other traditional systems, who continued to practice well into the later twentieth century. At the time Hoover built his house in Lincoln, practitioners of modernism in New England were rare; two of the most significant early houses, the Wells House in Southbridge and the Field House in Weston, were designed by architects—Paul Wood and Ned Goodell, respectively—who did very little after their groundbreaking work of the early 1930s. A third pioneer, Eleanor Raymond, left an impressive though more eclectic body of work that tended especially late in her career to intermix a careful updating of the Colonial Revival with a soft but sometimes technologically inspired modernism.

What turned Hoover to modernism, to what degree did the emerging vernacular of New England modernism in the postwar era affect his architectural outlook, and what influence in turn might Hoover have had on the evolution of modernism in this region? These are questions this book tries to answer. With the notable exceptions of Gropius, Marcel Breuer, and Walter Bogner, most of the architects who became Hoover's peers and competition in the postwar era were trained as modernists and therefore came to this way of design from the start, though it is important to remember that in terms of his built legacy, Hoover was never himself a "traditional" architect, with his first independent work being his own contemporary house in Lincoln.

As an architect who practiced most of his career alone and tended to remain (at least publicly) relatively aloof regarding contemporary theoretical debate, Hoover's embrace of modernism remains to some degree still a mystery, though it arguably grew in part out of his apprenticeship to landscape architect Fletcher Steele, from whom he developed a consequent appreciation of the intrinsic possibilities modernism held of a more intimate and symbiotic relationship between the natural and built environments. Steele was one of America's great twentieth-century landscape architects and theoreticians, who helped shepherd his discipline into the modern era. Works such as the Camden, Maine, Amphitheater and the gardens at Naumkeag in Stockbridge, Massachusetts, are both components in larger ensembles that include Colonial Revival and Shingle Style buildings and gardens, but they display a strong modern sense of space and form that emerges from rather than breaking with landscape tradition. Hoover was at Steele's side and highly engaged in this work while this transition was underway—the famous Blue Steps at Naumkeag are drawn in Hoover's hand, and he doubtless had a role in their design—and we can speculate with some certainty that the thought that went into this process may have had a profound influence upon Hoover's perception of what constituted an appropriate contemporary design intervention—whether building or landscape form—into the New England landscape.

Modern architecture typically draws inspiration from many sources, distills them through the lens of the program and site, and ultimately, at its best, creates new, seemingly inevitable syntheses that balance each of these forces in equal measure. Hoover understood this almost instinctively, and his work, as the authors state, is very much of its time and place; in this sense it resembles the New England modern vernacular evident in the work of architects such as Breuer, Walter Pierce, Eliot Noyes, and Carl Koch. This is most noticeable in his material palette, which, on the exteriors of his postwar work, typically utilizes vertical board siding—whether flush or tongue and groove—and large expanses of fixed glass glazed directly into wooden framing members coupled with stock industrial steel operable sash. Inside he frequently utilized random flagstone flooring, with oak and linoleum for secondary and tertiary spaces, and a variety of natural wood or plaster walls and ceilings.

The character-defining features that distinguish Hoover's work are subtle; there are distinctive tropes that emerge with familiarity with the work, but they do not call out for attention as "signature" elements. The most characteristic traits arise from the relationship of the house to its site, and to the procession one undertakes to approach and move through the structure. Hoover is a master at fostering a sense of anticipation that relies on a modest entry experience that encourages penetration into the house, where from what the authors characterize as the "plan's singular viewpoint" the discovery of the generously glazed living spaces reveals both the volumetric richness of the unfolding interior and the intimate symbiosis of the house and the landscape.

Another important environmental consideration that increases the sustainability quotient of Hoover's houses is their relation to the sun, specifically the strategic use of overhangs to control insulation—keeping the sun out in the summer, and allowing it to penetrate well into the house in the winter. Hoover's early houses have flat roofs with cantilevered soffits to create the overhangs; by the mid-1950s he is also using low-slope roof forms similar to those found in Carl Koch's Tech-built (and ultimately Deck house) designs, but with an attention to both proportion and level of finish that distinguishes them from these more generic types. This is most dramatically displayed in the Germeshausen House of 1959, one of Hoover's most distinctive designs, where the clients, having requested something evocative of Hawaii, were presented with a house in which the dominance of the roof forms—broad overhangs and deep gable end projections—are meant to call to mind the expansive low-slope roofs typical of tropical architecture. There is, however, an exquisite proportional equilibrium in the massing of the volumes and in the balance of solid, void, wall, and roof. The detailing and slightly increased angle of the pitch of the roof begins also to evoke Japanese and Alpine precedents, and the total ensemble is then reworked into a new synthesis that is branded with Hoover's quiet but assured sensibility.

Henry Hoover was in a very real sense both a humanist and an environmentalist: his houses provide places that encourage community at the family level, but also accommodate the need for private space, and he creates these spaces, when necessary, with a bare minimum of means. His environmental awareness was perhaps focused through a different lens than that which drives sustainable design today, but its ultimate goal was in essence very similar—a light touch on the land and balance with nature. Alan Cole, who commissioned the house where my family has now lived for twenty-two years, talked of the hours that Hoover spent on the site at different times of day and in different climatic conditions, absorbing the *genius loci* of the place before ever suggesting possible designs for the house—a methodical, experiential approach that is anecdotally confirmed by other Hoover clients as well. In our case, what ultimately emerged, as it did in so many of his commissions, was a "small house for big people" thoroughly in sync with its surroundings, where both needs and aspirations were accommodated through a clever, seemingly effortless interweaving of airy, uplifting collective spaces with numerous modest but never cramped refuges for rest and contemplation. In this quality is embodied the enduring value of the best modern architecture and the genius of Henry Hoover.

David N. Fixler
FAIA

ACKNOWLEDGMENTS

This project of many years could not have happened without the kindness and generosity of many people and institutions.

First and foremost, we are grateful to owners of Hoover houses cited in the book who opened their houses to us: Davina Adler, Karen and Bruce Clarke, Zoltan and Cristina Csimma, Steven Corcoran, Philip DeNormandie, Paul Giese, Amir Hoveyda and Suzanne Grey, David Jeffries, Eduardo and Carol Morata, Brooks and Patricia Mostue, Arthur Nelson, Charles and Katherine Staples, Emily Wade, and Ann Wiedie and Keith Hartt. We are also grateful to several additional Hoover house owners, whom we were fortunate to be able to interview before their deaths: Barbara Schmertzler Osborne, Elizabeth Peavy, Charles Satterfield, Constance Shearer, and Jeptha Wade. And still others connected to Hoover houses gave us substantive help in various ways: Bruce Adler, Doug Clayton, David Fixler and Phyllis Halpern, Edgar Lee, Frances Nelson McSherry, Claire Pearmain, Cynthia Ritsher, John Ritsher, Abigail Shearer Robinson, Alvin Schmertzler, Barry and Judith Solar, Joseph and Christine Ward, Carroll Weaver, Connie Witherby, and Aida and Alfred Wong.

We also benefited from conversations with several architects who worked with Hoover in the Hoover and Hill offices: Robert Adams, Dorothy Atwood, John Miller, and Joan Wood. Others outside the firm also provided information about certain aspects of Hoover's practice: George Burnell, Robert Edwards, and Philip Kendrick. In addition, several residents of Lincoln, Massachusetts, provided us with useful information pertaining to Hoover: Karen Crane, Earl Midgley, Dana Robbat, and Ruth Wales. Patrick Rice produced valuable schematics of Hoover's designs.

We gratefully mention as well numerous individuals, whose expertise and their institutions helped make this publication possible: Jeffrey Ochsner, Professor of Architecture, University of Washington, Seattle; Kathryn Leonard, Conservation Supervisor, and Judith Johnson and J. P. Brigham, University of Washington Library Special Collections, Seattle; Beth Mosher, Associate Professor, Department of Industrial Design, Rhode Island School of Design, Providence; Andrew Martinez, Archivist, Rhode Island School of Design, Providence; Lorna Condon, Curator of Library and Archives, Historic New England, Boston, MA, and Joseph Cornish, Supervising Preservation Services Manager, Historic New England, Waltham, MA; Mark Wilson, Curator of Collections, The Trustees of Reservations, Stockbridge, MA, and Miriam Spectre, Archives, The Trustees of Reservations, Sharon, MA; Virginia Hunt, Associate University Archivist for Collection Management, Harvard University Archives, Cambridge, MA; Ines Zalduendo, Special Collections Archivist and Reference Librarian, Frances Loeb Library Special Collections, Harvard Graduate School of Design, Cambridge, MA; Nancy Hadley, Manager, Archives,

American Institute of Architects, Washington, DC; Stephen Weiter, Director, College Libraries, State University of New York, College of Environmental Science and Forestry, Syracuse; Molly Bedell, Bedell Docs, Newbury, MA; Charles Sullivan, Executive Director, Cambridge Historical Society, Cambridge, MA; Robin Karson, Executive Director, Library of American Landscape History, Amherst, MA; David Rash, Independent Scholar, Seattle, WA; and Gary Wolf, AIA, Architects, Inc., Boston, MA.

Assistance also came from the following special collections and libraries: Leslie Perrin Wilson, Concord Free Public Library Special Collections, Concord, MA; Elise Ciregna, Director of Sales and Marketing, Forest Hills Cemetery, Boston, MA; Kara Fossey, Groton Historical Society, Groton, MA; Marie Wasnock, Archivist, Lincoln Public Library, Lincoln, MA; and Nanci Young, Archivist, Smith College, Northampton, MA.

Lastly, we extend our particular gratitude to Elizabeth Grossman, Professor Emeritus, Architectural History, Rhode Island School of Design, Providence, whose encouragement from the project's inception and ongoing professional guidance provided much solid underpinning to our work.

We would like to add the following names of Hoover house owners and friends who made contributions in tribute to Henry B. Hoover and in memory of Paul Giese. On their behalf, we sincerely thank the following: Davina Adler; Bruce and Karen Clarke; DOCOMOMO US; Sandra and Jonathan Grindlay; Elizabeth Grossman and Baruch Kirschenbaum; Mary Ann Hales; Douglas and Susan Harding; George and Barbara Harris; Amir Hoveyda and Suzanne Grey; Katherine Mierzwa and Michael Gerstein; Joanna and Daniel Melone; Ed and Carol Morata; Brooks and Patricia Mostue; Arthur Nelson and Frances Nelson McSherry; John and Bettina Norton; Wanda and Frank Paik; Dana and Joseph Robbat; Barbara Slayter; Barry and Judith Solar; Mary and James Spindler; Dealton Smith and Nancy Lawrence; Charles and Katherine Staples; Emily Wade; Ruth Wales; Ann Wiedie and Keith Hartt. And to those generous donors whose support arrived after the printing of these pages, please know we are grateful to you all.

INTRODUCTION

An episode several years ago propelled us to write this book. An important house by Henry B. Hoover (1902–89) was then threatened with demolition.[1] The house was "saved."[2] But the threat made clear that in Massachusetts there was a marked lack of recognition of early modern architecture, apart from the work of famous practitioners such as Walter Gropius and Marcel Breuer. Both European architects, brought to Harvard by 1937, had worked in Lincoln, Massachusetts. Although Hoover's own earliest residential work in Lincoln predates that of Gropius as well as Breuer, Hoover's contribution to modernism has remained largely overlooked (Figure 1.1).

In recent years, respectful attention has increasingly been paid to early modern buildings in the United States and to the beginnings of North American modernism by various publications, such as *The Struggle for Modernism* by Anthony Alofsin on Harvard University's role in the promotion of modernism.[3] There has also been relatively steady interest in the breadth and depth of modern architecture of other parts of the country, particularly the West Coast and Midwest, with attention not only to the big names but also to less well published practitioners.[4] Certain areas of the East Coast, such as Sarasota and Miami, Florida, have also enjoyed some architectural recognition.[5]

In New England, however, despite the efforts of organizations and individual proselytizers, and a few publications, general awareness remains wanting.[6] This situation may have to do with the particular character of New England, with its long tradition of emulating and interpreting existing eighteenth- and nineteenth-century building forms and materials. Minimal interest may also be the result of absence of publications that point to and explicate the particular character of New England modern houses. These hypotheses seem to explain the lack of awareness and understanding of Henry Hoover's work.

Our book, examining Hoover's career as a modern architect based primarily in New England, is intended to address an unwarranted omission. Hoover's practice demonstrates how he utilized, transformed, and individualized prevailing Beaux-Arts architectural training of the 1920s (at the University of Washington and Harvard University) to achieve modern residential architecture informed by but different from the normative (Bauhaus driven) idea of modern architecture. Hoover's practice additionally provides a valuable example of the importance of the influence of landscape architecture on stylistic development. Because he worked with landscape architect Fletcher Steele for almost a decade, it is not surprising that in Hoover's residential architecture siting is paramount.[7] His clients were professionals, many of them academics as well as businessmen, who sought a particular synthesis of the exceptional and the livable in houses that spoke to and of the New England landscape and were tailored to their site. The story of Hoover's long career is therefore one of an American-trained architect

FIGURE I.1 Henry B. Hoover on site, ca. 1957. Gift of Barbara Schmertzler Osborne to Hoover Family. HBH Papers, Hoover Family.

who in the late 1930s initiated his "brand" of modern architecture in New England. His work matured in the 1950s and continued well into the third quarter of the twentieth century.

In this study we have used a number of criteria to select which works from his oeuvre to discuss. Some we chose for their place in his design development, others for their remarkable state of preservation, the documentation available, or their accessibility. We have visited each of them more than once, and in many cases we have had the privilege of conversations with the original client. In other cases we have benefited from talking with the present owners, who have often provided equally illuminating comments. One owner described the mise-en-scene Hoover had created for them. "The house's open, yet tranquil environment allows us to enjoy our typically long hours of writing and thinking. Especially when the weather is beautiful like now, we just look out the windows and feel instantly relaxed. . . . For us, it's the ideal house. . . . The house, as you can imagine, fires my imagination."[8] Befitting clients' recognition of his authority in the realm of design and his own dry sense of humor, Hoover was once addressed as "Trapelord."[9] In fact, he did in a sense "command" a highly respected architectural practice from his office in Lincoln on Trapelo Road.

Hoover's path led from Muscatine, Iowa, where he was born, to Boise, Idaho, where he grew up, to the University of Washington and on to Harvard University and New England, where he established his career. It flourished in the post–World War II era when affordability and restraint were not just necessities but given value, when design was equated with forward thinking rather than ostentation, when accommodation of a family's needs was an architect's genuine concern. In these respects, Hoover's modern residential architectural practice offers a history of attitudes worth recalling.

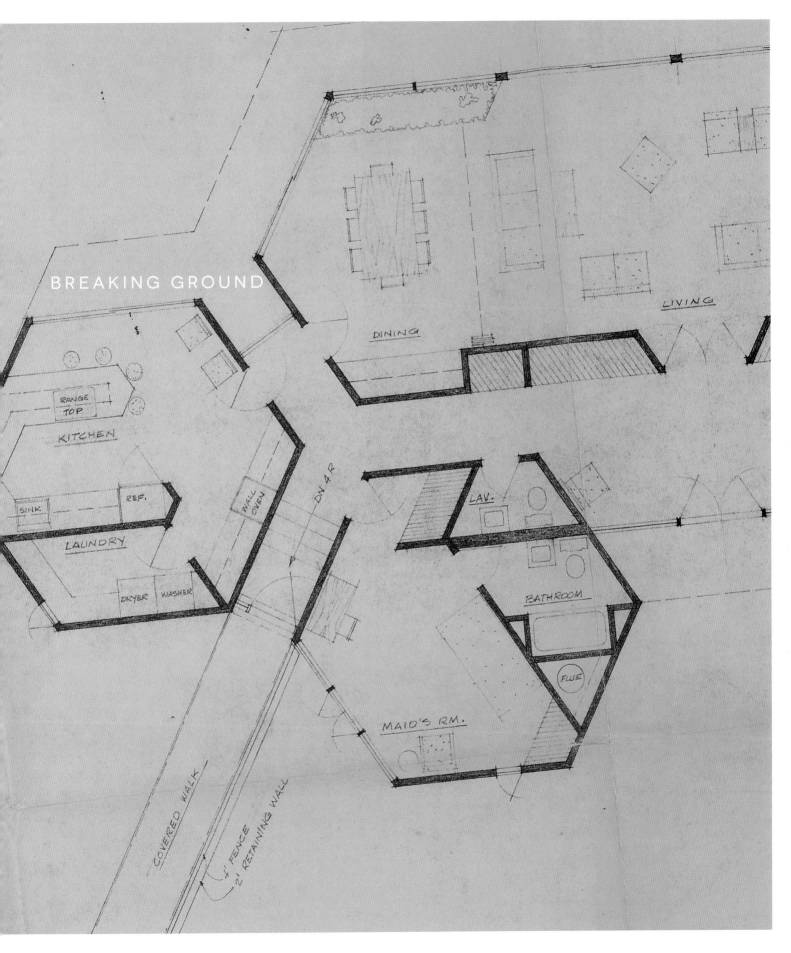

1 EDUCATION

Hoover "is thoroughly imbued with continuing in architecture as his life work, and I feel nothing would shake him from it."[1] Thus did Carl F. Gould, head of the Department of Architecture at the University of Washington, Seattle, refer to Henry B. Hoover (1902–89), when recommending him in 1924 to George H. Edgell, dean of the faculty of Harvard's School of Architecture, Cambridge, Massachusetts. Hoover had just received his B.A. cum laude in architecture from the University of Washington. The curriculum of that department under Gould was firmly tied to the École des Beaux-Arts system, and Harvard's too in the 1920s retained much of a Beaux-Arts tradition.[2] Yet, within the ten years after receiving his M.Arch. at Harvard and designing his first house in 1936–37, Hoover developed a distinctly modern vocabulary. Hardly alone in responding to "the modernist trend (shall I say revolution?)," as noted Beaux-Arts-trained architect Paul Cret put it in 1933, Hoover synthesized rigorous Beaux-Arts study with an interest in modernism to shape his own residential practice.[3] This chapter traces Hoover's passage from Beaux-Arts training at two important architectural schools to his contribution to "the gestation of modernism" in New England taking place within the context of the ongoing influence of avant-garde ideas.[4]

Hoover began studying architecture at the University of Washington in 1920. The department's architectural approach at that time is clear from the description for "Architecture Design" in the 1924–25 catalogue of instruction: "Most of the work is done under the programs of the Beaux Arts [sic] Institute of Design, New York, and is sent there for judgment where it is placed in competition with work of the leading schools of architecture in this country."[5] Gould, a New Yorker, and École- and Harvard-educated, had determined this direction when invited to head the university's new architectural program in 1914. And Gould was both an educator and a practicing architect, whose art deco Seattle Art Museum (1933) exemplifies a Beaux-Arts flexibility and receptivity to stylistic trends.

In 1925, on the tenth anniversary of the formation of the Department of Architecture, Gould further explained:

Our school is a professional school with a carefully devised and balanced educational ration worked out. The system we follow was evolved from one begun in the time of Louis XIV, taken over by the Society of Beaux-Arts Architects in New York City, and variously adapted by the major schools of architecture in this country. Our student pursues for a period of four years the study of one of the chief elements of human culture, and does his work under a discipline in which we strive to develop his faculties of both perception and creation. The programme and esquisse [sketch] as a base for our design problems are the foundations for the development of our course. Freehand drawing to train the hand and eye. Descriptive geometry to facilitate visualization. Mathematics and mechanics of

FIGURE 1.1 The Pantheon, Rome.
Hoover student drawing, ca. 1920–
23. HBH Papers, Hoover Family.

FIGURE 1.2 "Pantheon, Rome."
The University Prints, Boston (G87).
HBH Papers, Hoover Family.

materials to attain a structural understanding. History and theory to give background and a thoughtful attitude.[6]

An example of Hoover's "freehand drawing" is a rendering of the Pantheon (awarded an A), one of dozens of such drawings of notable structures and pieces of sculpture that Hoover kept, all of which received equally high grades (Figure 1.1).[7] The University Prints, Boston series, issued in the early twentieth century, provided the image source (Figure 1.2).

Although the department's program thus had solid pedagogic footing, it was less physically anchored, moving more than once before settling into the attic of Education Hall in 1922. This space, like others before it, was labeled "the Shack," a moniker that may explain Hoover's wry recollection of the department.[8] He characterized the department as a room filled with a few architectural magazines.[9] However, within this spare environment, students, Hoover included, gained a grounding in design, draftsmanship, mechanical/structural problems,

and some history and theory for "background" and "a thoughtful attitude."

Hoover's transcript includes courses in the "History of Architecture" extending to the Renaissance, according to the 1923–24 instruction catalogue, and courses in "Building Construction," "Freehand Drawing," "Sketches," and "Architectural Design" Grades I and II, in which "Work is done under the Society of Beaux Arts [sic] System."

Putting a Beaux-Arts curriculum of the early 1920s briefly in broader American context seems in order here. Arthur C. Weatherhead's history of architectural education in the United States (1941) and John F. Harbeson's more focused look at the Beaux-Arts Institute of Design program, which was established to support Beaux-Arts training in America (1927), are helpful in this regard. In Weatherhead's opinion, Beaux-Arts pedagogy was particularly evident in American architectural schools' emphasis on design and development of a "logical, well-organized and beautiful plan" that was "buildable." Construction methods mattered, though in education little consideration was given to "such factors as locality of site." In terms of design, the "formal and monumental" derived from the "Classic ideal" largely prevailed, requiring knowledge of historical architectural structures and motifs. Lastly, the student's design project was to be elaborately, indeed beautifully, rendered.[10]

Harbeson was more systematic in outlining the study of architectural design in the United States under the sway of the École des Beaux-Arts system. He therefore gave the Beaux-Arts Institute of Design, New York City, and its programs "special reference."[11] *The Study of Architectural Design* led a student step by step through methodology, critiques, scheduling, and problems on both Class B and Class A levels, involving character of plan, motifs, size, scale, and proportion. Class A problems were more advanced and more difficult, being either broader in scope or more focused in their study of a single building's plan.[12] For one Class A problem proposed by Harbeson, he pointed out that site could be among the "circumstances" making a symmetrical plan impossible. Other circumstances included complex or diverse programmatic requirements, though symmetry of "features and groups of features ... about minor axes" remained.[13]

Therefore, by considering the importance of site and of varying functions, Harbeson insisted on the challenges that students were required to meet. Furthermore, Harbeson in conclusion seemed to invite stylistic flexibility:

> We cannot do well in design without knowing something of the history of architecture and the growth of styles ... but must look for the interesting, the beautiful, the structurally satisfying qualities in each style. ... we must not with pre-conceived ideas ... look only at the accepted, the academic.[14]

He even mentioned an essay entitled "Modern Architecture" by his Beaux-Arts trained mentor, Paul Cret, though apparently not so much because of the topic's newness as for its part in the continuum of writings about what Harbeson called the underlying principles of architecture.[15] These principles were promoted by the Beaux-Arts Institute of Design and its "parent," the École des Beaux-Arts in Paris, the first architectural school, as contemporary architectural critic Paul Goldberger has labeled it.[16]

By the early part of the twentieth century, the Beaux-Arts Institute of Design began to hold project (programme) competitions in New York City for students in architectural schools all over the country. The University of Washington had subscribed by 1915–16.[17] In these competitions, students might receive medals or mentions. Seven examples of drawings and watercolors from Hoover's student days have survived, including one stamped twice with Beaux-Arts Institute of Design seals (Figs. 1.3, 1.4).[18] He won second mentions and one first mention.[19]

Hoover entered Harvard University in 1924 and received his M.Arch. there in 1926. In other words, he studied at Harvard more than a decade before Bauhaus founder and architect Walter Gropius became chair of the Department of Architecture in the Graduate School of Design, an appointment that underscored the department's ideological turn to a modernism implacably opposed to the Beaux-Arts. What would Hoover have learned at pre-Gropius Harvard? Edgell, dean of the faculty of architecture and landscape architecture, upon his appointment in 1922 made an attempt to "confront the changing academic perceptions of modern architecture," according to Anthony Alofsin.[20] As Edgell's writings indicate, he advanced interest in and understanding of new materials, technology, and engineering, and the exploration of a modern design vocabulary. Indeed, Hoover's "thesis construction," dated March 20, 1926, contains plans (no elevations) for the first and second floors of "A Laboratory Theatre" and more than seventy sheets

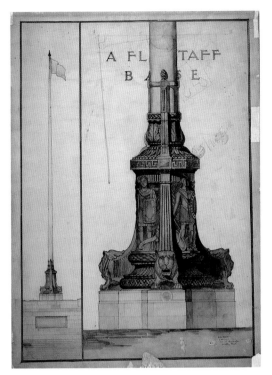

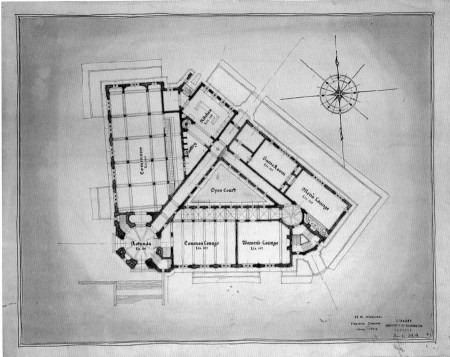

of construction details.[21] On these pages are noted materials such as "Berloy," pyrobar roof tile, and concrete.[22] Edgell was also instrumental in encouraging more modest and less monumental projects, fostering occasional collaborations between architecture and landscape architecture, and developing a graduate program in city planning. Most significantly, under Edgell, the focus of study in the department shifted from "history to an emphasis on design."[23]

Edgell authored a number of books on architectural history. Hoover owned a copy of Edgell's first, *A History of Architecture* (1918), coauthored with Fiske Kimball.[24] The result was the "first such survey written in the United States."[25] Its chapters reflected the authors' specialties. According to the Authors' Preface, chapters VI to IX on medieval architecture were Edgell's; those on "ancient and modern times" as well as "Eastern Architecture" were Kimball's.[26] Hoover could have acquired his copy while still an undergraduate studying architecture at the University of Washington or after he entered Harvard. Whatever the case, he printed out his name "H.B. Hoover" twice on the cover page.[27]

Kimball's chapter devoted to "Modern Architecture" begins with the mid-eighteenth century, extending well into the nineteenth, when Kimball says "the marvelous material development . . . introduced a body of architecture which, in spite of its variety, has a fundamental unity in its striving for functional expression." He goes on to discuss the impact of "functionalism" on the use of materials such as iron, glass, stone, Ferro-concrete, and the development of types

FIGURE 1.3 (*left*) "A Flagstaff Base," Hoover competition drawing, ca. 1923–24. University of Washington Libraries, Special Collections uw36303.

FIGURE 1.4 (*right*) Thesis Design, Hoover drawing, 1924. University of Washington Libraries, Special Collections uw36304.

of structures.[28] In the following chapter on "American Architecture," as Kimball turns to the early twentieth century, a penciled-in elongated check mark appears in Hoover's copy beside the word "functionalism."[29] A few pages later, Kimball introduces Louis Sullivan's Transportation Building at the Chicago Exposition (1893) and Frank Lloyd Wright's Unity Church (1908), under the header "modernist forms," praising Wright's use in his residential designs of

> broad ramified plans, wide eaves, novel fenestration, and a harmonious use of abstract motives of ornament, which have a suggestion of the Japanese. The appropriateness of these houses to the landscape of the lakes and the plains has been widely recognized.[30]

In the end, though, Kimball wonders whether the "neoclassical tendency" evident at the 1893 Exposition will prevail "or whether the international forces of functionalism will ultimately cause a wider adoption of modernist forms."[31]

Ten years later, Edgell appears to answer this question in his own book *The American Architecture of To-day,* published in 1928, that deals much more fully with modern American architecture. However, he identifies it broadly and conventionally as whatever had been "recently built or is being built to-day."[32] Within this definition, he positions various historicizing and local architectural tendencies as well as those associated with the "aesthetic ideas of Louis Sullivan and Frank Lloyd Wright." It is a "new movement . . . still in an early evolutionary stage" that, though "hard to define . . . is the spokesman of 'modernism' in the United States."[33] Edgell works to explain. It "stands for something new," he writes, in the use of concrete and steel and consists of

> large masses, of rectangularity, of generally horizontal emphasis. Its forms are kept as simple as possible, ap-

parently to drive home upon the observer the character of the forms themselves. It is an architecture which of course scrupulously avoids any similarity with past styles.[34]

Edgell related "the modernistic movement" in the United States to that in Scandinavia and to French *arte moderne,* as well as the interesting and sometimes "bizarre" work produced in Germany and the Netherlands.[35] First presented in 1927 as a series of three lectures on American modern architecture at the Henry La Barre Jayne Foundation in Philadelphia, the text may be read as indicative of normative ideas about modernism at Harvard's School of Architecture under Edgell's deanship during the time Hoover studied there.

According to the *Official Register of Harvard University,* the course Edgell taught with Kenneth J. Conant as early as the mid-1920s, "History of Medieval, Renaissance and Modern Architecture," included "very briefly the tendencies of modern architecture."[36] By 1934, his attention had broadened somewhat. His syllabus for "Fine Arts 1b" (given differently in the School of Architecture as 1c) listed the following buildings under the header "Modernist American Architecture": Sullivan's Transportation Building, Chicago (1893); Wright's Coonley House, Riverside, Illinois (1908), and Imperial Hotel, Tokyo (1916); Goodhue's Nebraska State Capitol (1922–23); Hood's Chicago Tribune Building (1925), American Radiator Building (1924), Daily News Building (1930), and Radio City RCA Building (1932). Two of these buildings—Wright's Coonley House and Imperial Hotel—had earlier appeared in Edgell's 1928 *The Architecture of America To-day.*[37] His greater awareness and evolving taste is suggested by mention in his 1934 syllabus of buildings by German, French, Spanish, and Dutch "modern" architects, among them Gropius, Oud, and Le Corbusier.[38] But he does not mention Howe & Lescaze's Philadelphia Savings Fund Society Building (1930–32) or more recent Wright buildings. Hoover's transcripts at Harvard indicate that he took Edgell's architectural history course in 1925 and received an A.[39]

The other member of the architectural faculty at Harvard who surely influenced Hoover was Jean-Jacques Haffner, hired by Edgell as the Nelson Robinson professor of design in 1922. Haffner, French-born and École des Beaux-Arts trained, had won the Grand Prix de Rome only three years before his appointment to the Harvard Faculty of Architecture. As professor of design, Haffner taught "Theory of Architecture 10," described in 1926 as a "series of talks and criticisms, in relation to the current problems, on elements of architecture, methods of working, principles of composition, decoration, etc."[40] Hoover's transcript indicates that he took the course. Its references to "current problems … elements of architecture, methods of working, principles of composition" come straight out of Beaux-Arts pedagogy.[41] However, Haffner's position was that new materials and new forms led to new solutions and were important "in the development of the new architecture," to use Haffner's words.[42] These were the sources of architectural change. An architectural contemporary praised Haffner's logic (perhaps a synonym for rigorous Beaux-Arts training) as a "French architect" but also his ability to train others to "recognize the individual peculiarity inherent to each problem."[43] In choosing words to recommend Hoover for a Sheldon Fellowship in 1926, Haffner wrote of him as having "a feeling for architectural detail which he always combines with general structural ideas to achieve the most brilliant solutions."[44] Hoover could also render them brilliantly; he became the first winner upon graduation of Harvard's Eugene Dodd Medal for excellence in freehand drawing and watercolor.[45]

In 1929–30, Haffner lectured on modern architecture in Boston, Chicago, and Washington, DC, under the auspices of the Cambridge School of Domestic Architecture and Landscape Architecture. According to printed extracts of these lectures, Haffner reiterated Edgell's opinion about Wright, declaring him as one who "stands out for his creative work far above any architect of his time." No doubt he also admired Wright for his integration of house and garden. Haffner emphasized this aspect of design in his announcement for the lectures. His pictorial "call to arms" for "the modern house with the Landscape treatment seen below" displayed a flat-roofed house with its planes punctured asymmetrically by sizable glazed vertical and horizontal areas, in three-quarter view, completely surrounded by stylized vegetation.[46] A similar vignette, appropriately printed in verdant green, served as the frontispiece for Haffner's *Compositions de jardins* of 1931, a compilation of his lectures.[47] In that publication, Haffner stated:

> The mass of the house, delightful and impressive through its domination, handling and relation of planes and volumes, of solid walls and openings, will transmit to the garden treatment this same relation and balance of volumes. Planes limiting the volumes will continue and prolong the impression of quietness, neatness, and rest of the architecture to the outdoor spaces and garden features.[48]

Architecture and landscape design are here brought together in words as Haffner positioned them visually in his vignette.

Haffner was joined on the Cambridge School of Architecture and Landscape Architecture lecture circuit by landscape architect Fletcher Steele, who spoke on modern gardens. Coming from a horticultural background, Steele had undertaken graduate work at Harvard's then recently established School of Landscape Architecture in 1906–7.[49] His instructors included Frederick Law Olmsted, Jr., and Arthur Shurcliff. He did not complete the program, choosing instead a six-year apprenticeship with Boston landscape architecture Warren H. Manning, one of the eleven founders of the American Society of

Landscape Architects. Nevertheless, Steele remained on the landscape architecture department's guest lecturer/critic circuit and was well known to Harvard faculty. By 1915, Steele had his own practice. His firm flourished during the 1920s and 1930s, surviving both the Depression and World War II, essentially concluding with one "last big garden" in 1963–68.[50]

Perhaps Haffner's emphasis on landscape and architecture influenced Hoover's decision to work with Steele in 1925 while he was still studying at Harvard. Exactly how the initial contact of Steele and Hoover was made is uncertain, but Hoover's Harvard "Report on Standing" of 1925 provides his address as "c/o Fletcher Steele, Esq. / 7 Water St., Boston."[51] And that year Steele wrote gracefully to thank Hoover for his help with the Hopkins Memorial at Williams College, Williamstown, Massachusetts (Figure 1.5).[52] Hoover also contributed to another project in 1925, one for William Barbour of Bloomfield Hills, Maine, begun the year before.[53]

In 1926, Hoover interrupted his work with Steele for travel abroad for almost two years (1926–28) on the Frederick Sheldon and Nelson Robinson Fellowships he had been awarded upon his graduation from Harvard. Professor Haffner's prophecy for Hoover as he headed for Europe is useful to cite here:

> I can see in this young student a really brilliant future as an architect and I mean an architect worthy of the name, who will be an honour and a success in the profession in the States.[54]

On his departure, Hoover certainly had the support of his Harvard professors and while abroad the company of Harvard peers some of the time. One companion was J. Carol Fulkerson, who received his M.A. from Harvard in Landscape Architecture, the same year in which Hoover received his M.Arch. Hoover mentions Fulkerson specifically as "the Charles Eliot fellow from the landscape school with whom I'm now traveling," in a letter of July 1927, written from Italy to Dean Edgell.[55] Hoover's eleven letters sent back to Harvard allow a partial reconstruction of what Hoover saw and thought.[56]

Hoover visited historically significant as well as little known buildings and gardens in Italy, France, Germany, Spain, and England. His first destination was Rome. While at the American Academy in 1926, Hoover expressed some disappointment with a professor he heard there, who

> spoke, mainly of raising a bulwark against the swelling tide of modernists, holding fast to the principles of the Greeks—etc. I had thought that the department of sculpture and painting had seemed ahead of the architectural department here and represented perhaps by better men. I think I know the reason now."[57]

Hoover, couched in Edgell's moderated acceptance of modernism, clearly takes the side of the modern movement.

In Munich in 1927, after visiting what he described as "the annual modern art exhibition in Munich," Hoover again shows his interest in "modern" architecture. He found the exhibition

> a little disappointing in the architectural section; much of Germany's recent work is hardly what I consider modern. It still looks like stone construction or the same thing they've always done with different detail. However, most of it is very good looking and quite in harmony with existing work.[58]

Reconstructing what Hoover meant is problematic because no documentation of that exhibition has yet surfaced. It seems, however, that Hoover used the qualifier "hardly" to refer to continuation of stone-based proportions instead of those made possible by modern steel.[59] As for what was on exhibit, his characterizations suggest that he did not see photographs and/or plans of the most

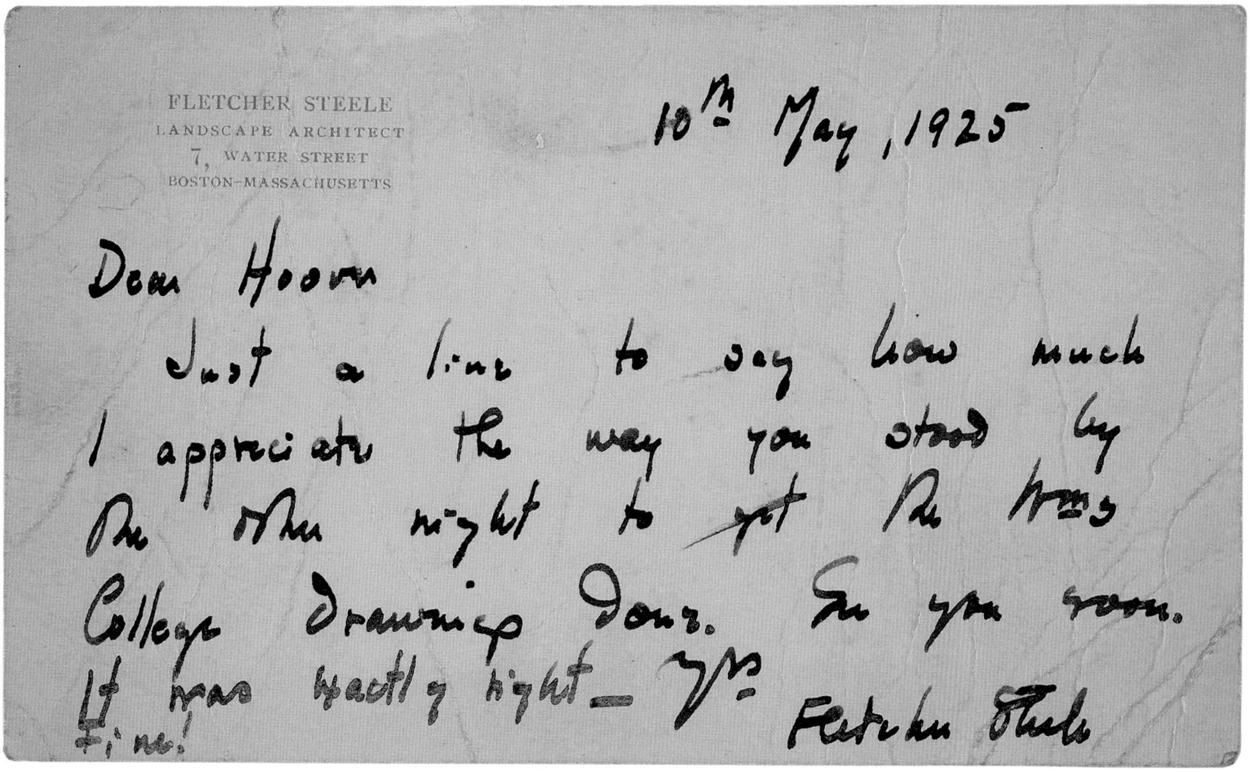

> FLETCHER STEELE
> LANDSCAPE ARCHITECT
> 7, WATER STREET
> BOSTON—MASSACHUSETTS
>
> 10ᵗʰ May, 1925
>
> Dear Hoover
>   Just a line to say how much
> I appreciate the way you stood by
> me the night to get the West
> College drawings done. See you soon.
> It was exactly right— Y⁰
>   Fletcher Steele
> fine!

FIGURE 1.5 Letter from Fletcher Steele to "Hoover," dated May 10, 1925. HBH Papers, Hoover Family.

recent avant-garde works such as the I. G. Farben Offices in Frankfurt (1927) by Peter Behrens and Erich Mendelsohn's Schocken Department Store in Stuttgart (1926). It is unlikely that examples of the Weissenhofsiedlung (1927) in Stuttgart by Le Corbusier, Mies van der Rohe, J. J. P. Oud, as well as Walter Gropius and Behrens, and of course the Bauhaus buildings by Gropius (1925) were included.

The word "modern" appears once more in a Hoover letter, this time of December 3, 1928, in reference to the Liverpool Anglican Cathedral (designed by Giles Gilbert Scott, foundation stone laid in 1904, not completed until 1980 by Scott's associates). It was, Hoover wrote, "not truly modern in the usual sense . . . more in the spirit of the great gothic buildings and surely more interesting than [Ralph Adams] Cram's (1863–1947) archeology [sic]." The use of that word suggests that Hoover had read Edgell's American Architecture of To-day carefully. There Edgell explained that modernism's practitioners "have a horror of the use of archaeological, or as they would put it, stolen forms," which Cram, who favored the Gothic style, did not shrink from doing.[60]

Hoover also noted other aspects of architecture when studying historic buildings. For example, when visiting Cordoba, Spain, in 1928, Hoover praised

FIGURE 1.6 Bernini's St. Peter's Piazza, Hoover Fellowship drawing, ca. 1927. HBH Papers, Hoover Family.

narrow streets opening now and then into little parks or gardens, through every doorway a glimpse of a patio filled with vines and plants, such a pleasing relation between architecture and planting. The same relationship is, I think the most attractive thing about the mosque itself and must have been even more pronounced originally. I wonder why we never do anything like that.[61]

And to him,

The English gothic [sic] cathedrals are charming but so much of that charm seems to depend on their situation. For me even Lincoln has not the feeling of the French ones. So often the proportions are unpleasing and the ornament is applied so that it hinders instead of heightens the effect.[62]

In 1927 when viewing the Tuilleries gardens, Hoover understood that

> Surely the Louvre, the Place de la Concorde, and the whole Champs Elysee through the Rond Point to the Etoile are as much a part of that garden as the flowers—a lesson in design all laid out of [sic] the ground, as well as one of the most attractive plans I know.[63]

The operative words here are "relationship," "situation," and "a lesson in design," involving in each instance both building and exterior space. Another example of this interaction, drawn but not mentioned specifically that way by Hoover in a letter, is one of the most notable architecturally encompassed spaces in the world, Gian Lorenzo Bernini's St. Peter's Piazza in Rome (Figure 1.6).[64]

It is notable that Hoover did not mention any avant-garde modern buildings in his correspondence to Edgell from Europe. Perhaps he did not seek them out as had Eleanor Raymond, to cite another American architect traveling in Europe in 1928, or the Harvard-educated architect Henry-Russell Hitchcock, abroad 1927–28, whose article on "Six Modern European Houses That Represent Current Tendencies in France and Germany" for *The House Beautiful* in 1928 includes works he would later characterize as International Style.[65] Hitchcock's ideas on the subject became codified in 1932 with the publication of *The International Style: Architecture since 1922*, which Hitchcock wrote with Philip Johnson.

Hoover, though receptive to modern architecture, does not seem to have been "converted" by his travels to an avant-garde approach to modernism. Instead, his letters affirm his exploration of the lessons he had learned at Harvard about what might be considered characteristic of modern architecture. That is, he was interested in modern materials, the proportions of buildings and gardens, and architecture's spatial relationship to site.

Perhaps these concerns help to explain why after his travels in Europe, Hoover rejoined landscape architect Fletcher Steele.[66] An unidentified newspaper notice entitled "Boise Boys: What They're Doing Now," postdating Hoover's M.Arch. degree and return home, described Hoover as "in charge of their [Steele's] new department of architecture and design."[67] Robin Karson identifies his last project with Steele as the Orchid Room garden room for Mrs. Randal Morgan (1938–40, Chestnut Hill, Pennsylvania), although drawings unmistakably in Hoover's hand for the Stanley Backus estate project (1940–42, Grosse Pointe Shores, Michigan) indicate that Hoover's association with Steele lasted at least until then.[68]

In fact, Hoover did not abandon his "faith" in architecture that long. Hoover's own 1932 characterization was that of "An apostate associated with a landscape architect, Fletcher Steele, and having a grand time designing anything from domestic architecture through rose gardens to silverware, garden sculpture, contemporary interior and furniture on the side."[69] Here Hoover wryly but pointedly itemizes what he brought to Steele's practice, which in fact was what he would bring to his own. It may be that Hoover was already thinking about moving on in 1932. Or Hoover may have been referring to the anomalous situation of an architect starting his career in the office of a landscape architect.[70] In any case, Hoover would become a fulltime architect before the forties and in a manner not derivative of International Style ideas.

By the time Hoover initiated his residential practice, his sensibilities as well as his knowledge base had been undoubtedly informed by his years with Steele. If Steele's garden designs did "constitute a link, arguably *the* link, between nineteenth-century Beaux-Arts formalism and modern landscape design," Steele's importance for Hoover can be understood.[1] Hoover made the same link when he took up residential architecture. Steele may have shown Hoover the way.

Steele was up-to-date on both modern French architecture and landscape architecture. He had attended the 1925 Exposition des Arts Decoratifs in Paris and came home excited by the modern landscape design and architecture on display. That exhibition influenced his ideas about form and space, and axial principles. In an article "New Pioneering in Garden Design," which appeared in *Landscape Architecture* in April 1930, Steele praised the work of modern French landscape architects. Among those cited was Tony Garnier, whose notions of space being separated by function are said to have influenced modern architects. Steele credited Garnier with starting "the strong modern trend away from symmetrical axial treatment. . . . formal lines and masses are in fact occultly balanced on an axis which is broken again and again, although rarely lost." He then suggested that what interested him most in the "poorly termed 'modernism,'" is "the expanded sense,—not a new sense but the expansion of our old sense of dimensions, space, relativity, call it what you will."[2]

Steele illustrated the article with photographs not only of gardens but also of houses by architects such as Le Corbusier, André Lurçat, and Gabriel Guevrekian (only one building is directly attributed in the text, and that to Lurçat). The structures are notable for their flat roofs and planar surfaces without ornamentation, large window areas, and what Steele termed "ceilings" extending over gardens "practically without posts so that one gets a strong sense of the garden boundary over one's head because of the contrast between such ceilings and, elsewhere, the open sky. This again emphasizes three-dimensional volume outdoors in buildings."[3]

Two years later in "Landscape Design of the Future," also for *Landscape Architecture,* Steele asserted: "In my opinion, the architect is primarily interested in the objects which he is designing; the landscape architect with the relation of things and the compositions of the spaces *between* them."[4] The emphasis is Steele's. How similar this sounds to observations Hoover made in his own writing on the subject in letters to Edgell from Europe.

Steele was particularly sensitive to vistas. Speaking of what may be his most famous work, he wrote, "After all, the view controls all design at Naumkeag."[5] He was even more expansive in a 1950 letter about the garden to his sister. He explained: "The vital importance of surviving form which was begun on the south lawn here at Naumkeag generated by the curve of Bear Mountain beyond and made clear in the curve cut in the woodland, was a satisfactory experiment. So far as I know it was the first attempt that has ever been made to incorporate the form of background topography into foreground details in a united design. Due to the limitations of the site, these particular convolutions could go farther than the drive on one side and the Perugino View on the other" (Figure 2.1).[6] A slightly more southward vista from the upper terrace affected another section of the garden. Steele designed an overlook onto distant, undulating Monument Mountain range, which he specifically identified on a garden diagram as "Perugino View." Hoover depicted this controlled vista in a drawing of November 1931.[7]

Robin Karson, in her monograph on Fletcher Steele, underscores Hoover's importance for Steele's practice in the several pages she devotes to "Henry Hoover and the Office."[8] A note from Steele dated 1932 gives some inkling of early procedures:[9]

Dear Harry [Henry Hoover]

Try a sketch of Backus piers [Stanley Backus project, Grosse Pointe Shores, Michigan] in form of very shallow sentry box—no door—on as near old pier design foundations as possible. Just big enough opening for man to stand in out of rain. Tudor feeling gotten by buttresses, perhaps or suggestions of battlements or little

FIGURE 2.1 "The Perugino View," Naumkeag, Hoover drawing for Fletcher Steele, 1931. Courtesy of the Terence J. Hoverter Archives, Moon Library, SUNY, College of Environmental Science and Forestry.

carving-like entrance door of house. Perhaps top of little gate to service could be hinted at in opening or something of same period. Don't want to work that motive too hard or will spoil gate. Flat arch like windows probably better. Stone back on Basecourt side. Suggestion of dovecote over if you want it, though probably too gardenesque, though carrier pigeons. & falcons were kept somewhere, surely.[10]

Clearly, Hoover's draftsmanship proved enormously helpful to Steele; his drawings were "utterly consistent: his forms were solid, his surfaces lively, and best of all for Steele's business, the pencil sketches were convincing."[11] But Hoover "proved an agile designer as well as draftsman, and Steele soon looked to him for new ideas . . . letting him develop designs at his own pace and rework them according to his own judgment."[12] Steele trusted Hoover's skill and judgment, giving him flexibility and expecting initiative. It is likely that Hoover did more than merely flesh out Steele's concepts, though the extent to which that happened remains undetermined.[13]

Hoover's work with Steele took place largely between 1929, after he had returned from his honeymoon in Europe and begun a full-time association, and 1937, the year Hoover's first residential design was completed. This time frame is reinforced by reproductions in Hoover's files of some of the drawings he made for Steele, including two originals found among Hoover's papers (Figure 2.2).[14] Judging from their dates, the years 1931–32 mark the apogee of the work Hoover did with Steele. Perhaps the Great Depression lessened demand for the luxury of these gardens replete with follies and gazebos, balustrades and ornamental paving, and perhaps Hoover was already beginning to think about starting out on his own. While the drawings in the files do not by any means represent the extent of Hoover's production for Steele—Karson's illustrations of drawings recognizably in Hoover's hand give proof of that—they do give some

sense of the importance of those years for the firm and for Hoover.

Of all of Steele's projects, Hoover seems to have identified most with Naumkeag.[15] The words "Naumkeag work" heads a list of projects that Hoover dictated late in his career. However incomplete this record is, it is clear that Naumkeag came first to Hoover's mind. Hoover spoke of one specific colleague sculptor, Archangelo Cascieri, whose skillful work in "creating" the Venetian posts for the Afternoon Garden at Naumkeag, the estate of Mabel Choate in Stockbridge, Massachusetts, had impressed Hoover.[16] He also described with satisfaction use of black glass to line the garden's shallow pools, thereby creating the impression of depth. At an early stage in its development, Hoover had drawn a "perspective plan . . . prepared for Paris Exhibition, 1930" of the Afternoon Garden and nearby cascading steps.[17]

But it was for the 1938 intervention in the landscape, The Blue Steps—four levels of double-sided steps with a curving railing that joins the upper garden to the wilder lower field—that Hoover seems to have played a major design role.[18] Hoover's June 1938 informal, nonpresentation sketch for the "Stairs down the Bank / Estate of Mrs [sic] Mabel Choate / Stockbridge Massachusetts," does not show the railing. However, his drawing of September 13, 1938, labeled "PLAN OF LEFT SIDE / RIGHT SIDE REPEATS IN REVERSE / SEE NOTE REGARDING EXCEPTION" is an elegantly rendered segment (Figure 2.3).[19] The drawing focuses on the curved railing in both end and side elevation and plan. Interestingly, Steele's subsequent written description of the steps' basic configuration (levels and turns and arched openings) makes no mention of the staircase's signature flowing railing.[20] Nor did he foreground the signature railing in the short piece he wrote almost a decade later on Naumkeag (Figure 2.4). Whether his silence means that the design was Hoover's is not clear. The illustration caption simply reads "the modern steps, painted blue."[21]

Fig 2.2 Memorial for Mrs. John Forbes, Hoover drawing, 1932. HBH Papers, Hoover Family.

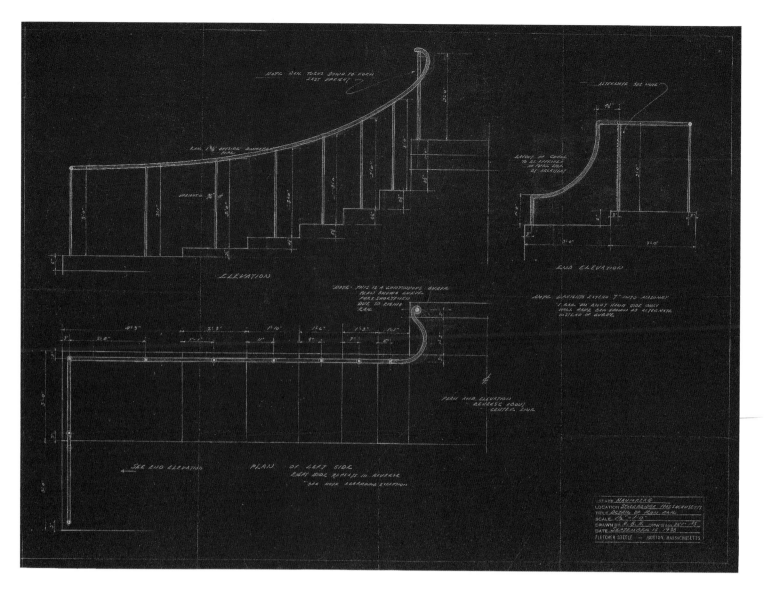

FIGURE 2.3 "Plan of Left Side" of the Blue Steps, Naumkeag, Hoover drawing, dated September 13, 1938. The Trustees of Reservations, Archives and Research Center, Sharon, MA.

Whatever the case, the structural concept and actual construction of the steps were surely Hoover's responsibility. Numerous detailed construction drawings by Hoover of the steps' "platform and ramp," "cinder block walls," "side footing," "step gutter," and so forth, survive.[22] In some cases, these plans contain annotations in red, added by Hoover, itemizing certain later changes. Hoover's skill as a designer and his knowledge of construction served Steele well. Years later, Hoover asserted that Steele

could not understand the principle of a catenary curve. When I demonstrated the contour of a swag chain by holding a piece of string, he objected that 'Chain behaves differently. It's heavier.' Once he designed a ten-foot aquarium wall that was completely impractical. I tried to explain surface pressure to him but he refused to believe that what he was proposing simply wouldn't work.[23]

It is tempting to suppose that Hoover's abilities helped bring into being the concepts Steele poetically expressed in his 1964 publication on *Gardens and People*:

> Garden steps should be plastic.... A hint of movement, of grace promised, of beauty that hides or lies forgotten. It is the curve of the back of a leopard made clear in the rail of a stair.[24]

Karson, in crediting Steele's landscaped gardens with remarkable spatial clarity and surprise, could just as well have been speaking of the houses Hoover would design. The notion of vertical as well as horizontal space integrating inside and out would also become central to Hoover's architectural design. And Steele's statements about nonaxial arrangement and perceived space as well as his penchant, observed by Karson, to "enhance space though illusion" in his garden designs are ideas that resonate in Hoover's later architectural work.[25]

What had shaped Hoover up to this point were professional forces. His solid Beaux-Arts background at the University of Washington and Harvard's School of Architecture became "part of what made Hoover a good architect, aware of what he was doing and in control of what he was doing," as an architect/draftsman associated with Hoover in the 1960s put it.[26] At Harvard, Hoover had benefited from professors such as Edgell and Haffner, appreciative of the potentials of new materials and technology and their impact on modern design, and in the importance of the role of landscape design. Harvard also, importantly, offered Hoover the opportunity to travel firsthand. Steele's own stated modus operandum—"to balance three tensions. The pull of the land. The pull of the client and the pull of the professional designer himself"—could be said to be Hoover's as well.[27] All of these personalities, opportunities, and experiences formed the bedrock for Hoover's architectural career.

FIGURE 2.4 Blue Steps, Naumkeag. HBH Papers, Hoover Family. Courtesy of Paul Giese.

In 1936, while still working for Steele but years after leaving Harvard, Hoover received an invitation from Joseph Hudnut, dean of the Graduate School of Design, to apply for the Arthur W. Wheelwright Traveling Fellowship.[1] It was not until April 1938, however, that Hoover submitted his application, apologizing for being "so slow in getting this in, and so much of the material I intended to use for its preparation was lacking that I have had to make it very general."[2] Perhaps ongoing work with Steele is one explanation for Hoover's lateness. In any case, he described the project as "An investigation of contemporary structural technique in Europe and the United States, with the intent to indicating possible improvements in the industrial design of fabricated building materials and equipment."[3] The fellowship, which had been established in 1935, was to fund travel and study in architecture outside the United States. Hoover's stated focus in his application indicates his own particular interest in modern structural matters and building materials. However, his very late formal submission surely diminished his chances, although at the end of April 1938, Hoover was notified, at Steele's business address as before, that he had been among the finalists. Indeed, Hudnut responded, "I hope that you will permit us to consider you next year in connection with this award."[4]

Hoover's ambitions are evident, but increasing economic and political turmoil at home and abroad may have dissuaded him. And, too, his personal situation—a growing family—would have made extended travel from home problematic. Most important, he had discovered Lincoln, Massachusetts, then still rural with available, reasonably priced land, a place where his keen interest in landscape could be coordinated with house design. Arguably, of all the fortunate circumstances of Hoover's early career, his discovery of this town and his decision to settle and establish a practice there, can be considered the most defining.

As early as 1935, Hoover had begun to consider his first independent residential project, a house for his family (1936–37, 1955). An elegant graphite sketch on tracing paper bearing the annotation "View from Living Court / House of Henry B. Hoover / at Lincoln Massachusetts / H. B. Hoover Architect July 1935" documents his ideas at the time (Figure 3.1).[5] This drawing shows a one-story, flat-roofed house with large, distinctly gridded, glazed facade of "large voids at the center and corners," interspersed by blank walls that overlook a terrace demarcated at one end by a garden wall ornamented with what appears to be an urn.[6] In exaggerated perspective, this rendering illustrates what would become one of the architectural ambitions of Hoover's work—"building and garden so perfectly blended that one is a part of the other."[7] The whole is a prefiguration, albeit with more vertical proportions, of the house that he would complete two years later. The "House of Henry B. Hoover" drawing is dated only two months after the birth of his first child on May

FIGURE 3.1 "View from Living Court." Hoover drawing, 1935. HBH Papers, Hoover Family.

16, 1935, suggesting a rationale for the seismic shift in Hoover's sense of himself and his design career—that is, his decision to practice architecture on his own rather than continue to work for Steele. That Hoover saved the ink-stained drawing, found only after his death, suggests its importance to him. In contrast, he never drew the "garden" he designed over his lifetime for his house; it was set to paper only after Hoover's death (Figure 3.2).[8]

According to land registration office records, Hoover had purchased land on Trapelo Road as early as 1934 and established a right of way from the public road at the same time. Years later he recalled coming to Lincoln from Cambridge, where he was then living, to scout out available property. He may have been prompted by somewhat earlier business trips for/with Steele to the town.[9] Whatever the case, finding a ridge that sloped steeply south, Hoover climbed a tree to see, a half-mile away through oaks and pine, a body of water known as the Cambridge Reservoir. He knew he had found his land. For two acres he paid $1,000.[10]

In 1936, Hoover began construction. As both client and architect, he had the opportunity to design exactly what he wanted for himself and his family and to respond as he wished to the land. At the same time his circumstances were constraining. Hoover had very little money. Banks were of little help. "The house was too far from the main road to be practical as a filling station (which the banks said was what it looked like), or was too small to be useful as a hospital which another bank said it resembled."[11] But the house was built. Hoover had undoubtedly walked his land as extensively as he would that of his later clients, investigating the site's natural

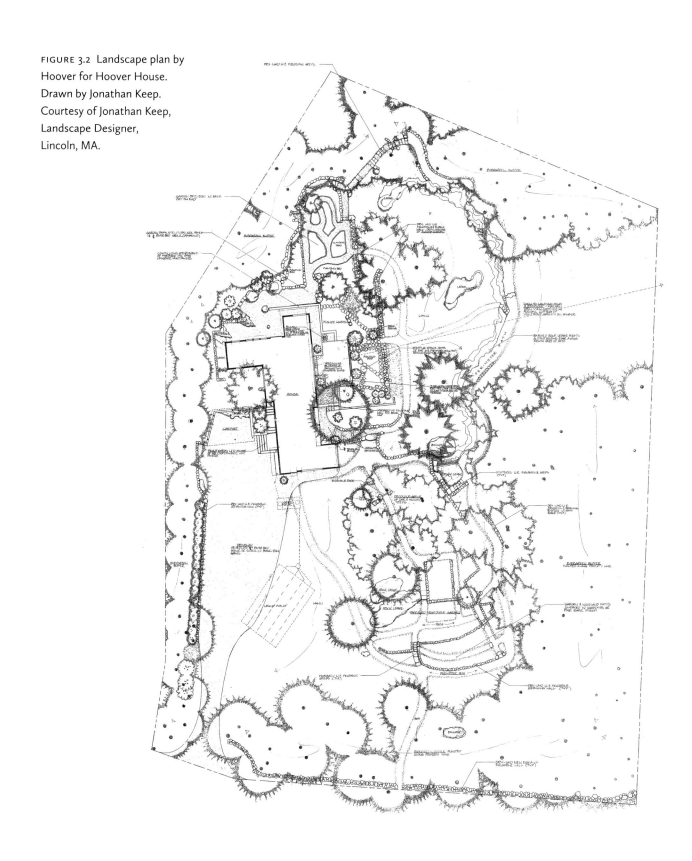

FIGURE 3.2 Landscape plan by
Hoover for Hoover House.
Drawn by Jonathan Keep.
Courtesy of Jonathan Keep,
Landscape Designer,
Lincoln, MA.

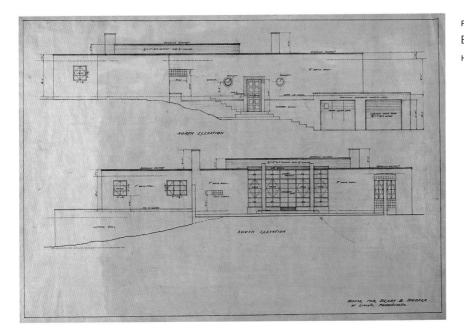

FIGURE 3.3 "North Elevation, South Elevation." Hoover drawing, ca. 1937. HBH Papers, Hoover Family.

contours and materials.[12] Like Steele, he treated the natural landscape as the elemental shaper of his design, having an uncanny sense of where a house would "grow" best, in this case between ledge outcroppings and a gentle westward slope, with the principal elevation facing south.

The HOOVER HOUSE (1936–37) is first seen upon the final turn of the driveway, the low and flat-roofed brick house consisting of two sections at right angles sited to give maximum exposure to sun and view.[13] Architecture like this had not been seen before in Lincoln. The north elevation was planar, largely without fenestration apart from two clear-glass round windows (each labeled "bullseye" on the plans) flanking the entrance and entry door set with eight translucent glass panels, and four square glass bricks ("glass inserts" on the plans), set into the wall.[14] In contrast to the opaque entrance facade, the south side became a gridded expanse of glass centered between blank walls. Above, the attic story and two imposing vertical posts startlingly countered the dramatic horizontality of lintel and window extension.[15] A single glass brick and chimney to the west and vertical window to the east challenged the south side's overall symmetry. The heavy lintel over the central windows and the narrower roof edge underscored the unity of the extended volume (Figure 3.3).

A short flight of interior stairs from the entry led to the modern great room of this nearly 1,800 square-foot house. Entrance was delayed actually and visually through the introduction of a right-hand turn at the top of the stairs. Only

FIGURE 3.4 South elevation, 1937
Hoover House. Period photograph.
HBH Papers, Hoover Family.

then in the central volume were the Reservoir and hills presented to the viewer. Hoover dramatized the scale of this room by raising the ceiling two-and-a-half feet above that of other parts of the house and by placing nearly twenty-seven feet of windows along the south wall (Figs. 3.4, 3.5). A fireplace wall, at cross axis to the view, opposed this outward focus. The other end of the room served as a dining room. Although the great room was not especially large (448 square feet), the vistas leading to the exterior and the careful delimiting of the volume to emphasize its ample proportions made it appear remarkably spacious. The private and service areas of the house lay east (study with two bedrooms and bath) and west (kitchen and additional bedroom and bath). Space given over to corridors was minimal, and those that existed were lit by small horizontal windows at eye level. The plan's logic, the sequestering of the private spaces, not only made the house highly livable for a family of two adults and three young children but also allowed the public room to function as an advertisement to clients of Hoover's skill in creating a modest house with volumetric generosity (Figure 3.6).

Hoover used lightly whitewashed, second-hand brick for exterior walls into which steel casement windows were set. Homasote particle board served as interior walls and asphalt tiles for the flooring.[16] These inexpensive materials reflected Hoover's limited funds and his innovative use of materials. With the exception of steel casement windows in the Gilboy House (q.v.), these materials would not reappear in Hoover's residential designs. Local symmetry and art deco detailing he also rejected in subsequent work.

On the other hand, Hoover exhibited for the first time what would be a life-long interest in the use of furnishings to define functional areas within a larger volume. It must be remembered that before World War II, there was no readily affordable commercial production of modern furniture in the United States.[17] Therefore, like other modern architects, Hoover chose to design his own. The rectilinear dining table of light birch with dark supporting wooden end panels connected by a metal rod; the round marble-top table with wooden tripod base;

FIGURE 3.5 Cambridge Reservoir from 1937 Hoover House. Period photograph. HBH Papers, Hoover Family.

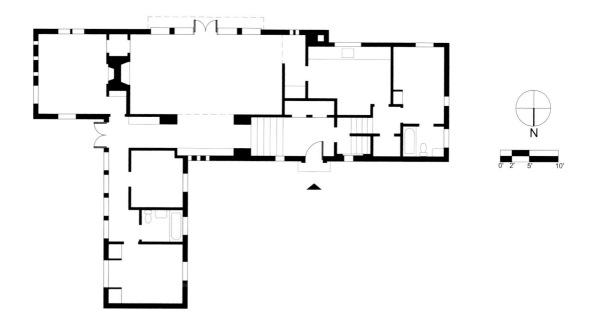

FIGURE 3.6 Plan of 1937 Hoover House. Drawn by Patrick Rice. HBH Papers, Hoover Family.

and the light birch bench are all Hoover's (Figure 3.7).[18] Their unadorned, simple lines and minimal mass enhanced the openness and scale of the great room.[19] Comparing Hoover's furnishings with other avant-garde interiors of the period, such as the "Living Room of a model apartment" in Zürich (1936) furnished by Marcel Breuer, or living spaces in "Windshield," the house designed by Richard Neutra (1936–38) for John Nicholas and Anne Brown off the coast of Rhode Island, it is apparent that Hoover was not interested in the shine of tubular steel or gravity-defining effects but on maximizing impact of volume.[20]

In 1955, a decade after the war, Hoover enlarged the house to approximately 2,700 square feet, reconfiguring the interior spaces and adding a two-bedroom wing to the west to accommodate his three children (Figure 3.8). The entrance area was pushed out and extended with floor-to-ceiling glazing, and the bullseye windows "separated" so that one remained in the exterior facade, the other absorbed into the interior entry. Inside, the delayed approach into the living room now received light from northern as well as southern exposure. The fireplace wall became asymmetrical by lengthening to the north. Hoover then upgraded the glazing along virtually the entire south wall, in this way emphasizing the expansiveness of the entire room and its connection with the landscape (Figure 3.9). A ten-foot glass slider set between floor-to-ceiling windows, nearly the length of the south elevation, replaced the former steel casement French doors. The height of the great room was lowered to accommodate new lighting in the

FIGURE 3.7 Interior showing
Hoover-designed marble-top table,
ca. 1937. Period photograph. HBH
Papers, Hoover Family.

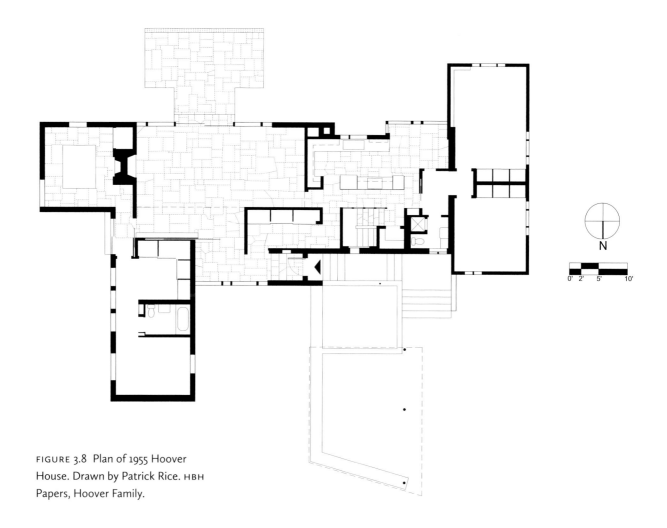

FIGURE 3.8 Plan of 1955 Hoover House. Drawn by Patrick Rice. HBH Papers, Hoover Family.

ceiling. Pickled vertical oak and fir siding and bluestone flooring in the great room and study replaced earlier modest materials. Continuing bluestone onto an outside terrace further emphasized the relationship between inside and outside living spaces.[21] The new two-car carport roofed with Visqueen added to the entrance side established a courtyard on approach.[22]

Years later, replying to his son's praise of his houses, Hoover, with typical understatement, wrote: "They are not innovative, hardly designed in a creative sense."[23] This appraisal is typical of his Beaux-Arts education, in which sense of the program and site as inspirational constraints were more important than the notion of individual genius and creativity. But Hoover was too modest. His 1937 house is in fact one of the two "first" modern houses in Lincoln.[24] Moreover, his 1955 modification exemplifies not only his postwar architectural thinking and willingness to update a house judiciously in response to new needs but also his ability to use the changes made to underscore the aspects of the original house that were most important to him. He made more emphatic the delayed entry into the living room and bond between house and landscape. In 2008, through a preservation easement with the Stewardship Program of Historic New England, Hoover's son and daughters ensured the house's perpetual protection.[25]

Within two years of building his own house, Hoover had received his first architectural commission from Glennon Gilboy, a professor of soil mechanics at the Massachusetts Institute of Technology; and his wife, Elizabeth Waterman Gilboy, an economist associated with various institutions including Harvard University. They had been renting a house on Trapelo Road in Lincoln but in 1937 decided to buy three and a third acres of land abutting Hoover's and asked him to design their home. In the architect's own words, Gilboy was his "1st real client / 1st house after ours / finished just before war."[26]

The GILBOY HOUSE (1939) commission offered Hoover an opportunity to design a house, this time larger (approximately 3,000 square feet) and more ambitious, for sympathetic clients (Figure 3.10). There is no extant record among Hoover's papers of the Gilboys' needs or desires for their house, so again Hoover started with the landscape.

The Gilboy land overlooked the same body of water that inspired the siting and

FIGURE 3.9 South elevation, 1955 Hoover House. Period photograph. Courtesy of Lincoln Town Archives, Lincoln, MA.

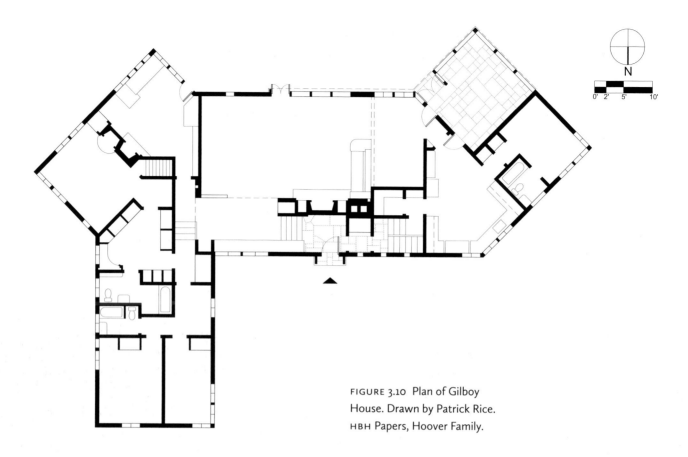

FIGURE 3.10 Plan of Gilboy
House. Drawn by Patrick Rice.
HBH Papers, Hoover Family.

design for Hoover's own house. As before, Hoover oriented the house to the south to frame the Reservoir view and maximize light. His careful siting also ensured that, despite their proximity, neither house intruded upon the other. Explaining how the house accommodates the sloping terrain, Hoover tellingly remarked that it "steps down the land."[27] As the house descends in section, Hoover extended the stone base of the house, which formed the long horizontal foundation of the garage wall and base of the house, vertically into the chimneys.

In the Gilboy House, he expanded on design elements he had used in his own. On approach, the view of the flat-roofed house is withheld until a final right turn of the driveway. However, the strict orthogonals of Hoover's own house are now obtuse angles, with "pavilions" splayed apart from the main volume. Placing the

study with sun porch above on one end of the central block and screened porch on the other at a slight angle gives these rooms optimum light and viewscape. The open-trapezoidal footprint shows Hoover's heightened confidence in design and the efforts to which he would go to integrate the house with the contours of the land. Volumes overlap and interlock in more elaborate balance as they assertively claim the site.[28]

Granite steps following the contour of the natural rock ledge form the approach to the house. The entry consists of a portico sided by three stacked translucent glass panels. The placement of windows to the left and right of the door is decidedly asymmetrical and serves to accentuate the horizontal tension and blankness of the facade (Figure 3.11). On the south, or Reservoir facade, however, a strong sense of symmetry is created by the

FIGURE 3.11 North elevation,
Gilboy House. Period
photograph. HBH Papers,
Hoover Family.

FIGURE 3.12 South elevation, Gilboy House. Period photograph. HBH Papers, Hoover Family.

balance of the canted porch and study wings framing the great room, the greater actual size of the porch being mitigated by its openness. The study/sundeck/chimney stack's verticality on one end and the heavy mullions in the great window and the lighter posts of the screened porch on the other, counter to some degree the house's overall horizontality. The extent of the window lintels and roofline spreads the house out between land and sky (Figure 3.12).[29]

The interior also retains characteristics of Hoover's 1937 house. From the entry hall a short set of stairs leads up to the living room. A turn at the top of the stairs opens to the view of the Reservoir through the south wall, which is glazed with fixed and operable steel-frame windows that are the full height of the facade and run nearly three-fourths the length of the room.[30] Again, the raised ceiling of the main living area allows Hoover to differentiate various areas of the volume while maintaining a sense of overall spaciousness and continuity. The space is defined by a fireplace wall, this time opposite the view, and by built-in sofa components at right angles to it, with a glass drum-top table nearby, all designed by Hoover (Figure 3.13).[31] Hoover's positioning of these components requires another turn to the right in order to re-experience the vista that was first viewed upon entering the living room. The dining space, for which Hoover designed a metal and wood table, was here demarcated by a lowered ceiling and curtain track. Parquet flooring was used in the main room, oak and linoleum elsewhere.[32]

Beyond the living area lie the private areas to the north and services to the east and west. In the private wing, bedrooms and a study (for which Hoover designed the desk and the master bedroom's closets and dressing table) are fitted into the splayed angle of the house plan.[33] The kitchen is formed by a similar *poche* in the service wing, accessed from the entry hall by a second set of steps that leads up to the kitchen, and the adjoining maid's room and down to the utilities and garage.[34]

Although the house has undergone some changes in the secondary areas, the public room remains essentially unchanged and the house's integrity unaffected. However, the horizontal siding was replaced with vertical boarding in the 1950s, which lessens the effect of the house hugging the ledge. The impact only points up Hoover's exploitation of materials (horizontally laid stone and wood) to achieve the integration of house and site that was so central to his work.

Hoover's first houses are undeniably in a modern idiom. Where might inspiration have come from, other than the limited perspective of Edgell at Harvard and Steele's awareness of French modernism and travels in Asia? The two major local exhibitions sponsored by the Harvard Society of Contemporary Art, Cambridge, Massachusetts, on Buckminster Fuller's Dymaxion House (May 1928) and on the Bauhaus (December 1930), an exhibition that spawned Hitchcock's and Johnson's international style exhibition at the Museum of Modern

FIGURE 3.13 Interior of Gilboy House with Hoover-designed furniture. Period photograph. HBH Papers, Hoover Family.

Art, New York City, in 1932, with its reiteration at Harvard's Fogg Art Museum, Cambridge, Massachusetts, the following year, do not seem to have definitively registered with Hoover. Information from publications on modernism and articles in architectural journals such as *Architectural Record, Architectural Forum,* and *House Beautiful* are more likely sources of ideas.[35] Another perspective could have come from Wright's lecture at Jordan Hall, Boston, in 1932 on new German architecture.[36]

On the other hand, the beginning of modernism in New England has been (in)famously pegged by Sigfried Giedion, secretary-general of the Congrés Internationaux d'Architecture Moderne (founded 1928), to the arrival of Gropius and Bauhaus pedagogy at Harvard. Giedion had been asked to present the Charles Eliot Norton Lectures in 1938–39 at Harvard upon Gropius's recommendation.[37] In his subsequent (1941) publication *Space, Time, and Architecture: The Growth of a New Tradition,* Giedion claimed that until 1938 and Gropius's "newly finished 'modern house' [in Lincoln, Massachusetts] . . . not a single example [of modernism] could be found within a radius of upwards a hundred miles."[38] He overlooked even earlier examples of modernism in New England.[39] The point is that Hoover's first two modern houses predate or postdate by just a year Gropius's own house in Lincoln. It is unlikely that either architect knew the other by 1937–39.

What other work Hoover was able to complete before World War II is unclear. The checklist he prepared intriguingly does include three clients' names between 1940 and 1942. These projects were almost surely executed, judging from Hoover's brief, cryptic comments on his checklist of projects, but nothing more is known about them. The name of a fourth, in contrast, is known only from existing plans for the ground and second floors: "Study House for E. M. Lowe / Portchester [*sic*] New York" by "Henry B. Hoover Architect / Boston Massachusetts Jan. 1941." It is likely that this house was never built. Hoover also added the annotations "morning sun / winter," "afternoon sun / winter" and "panoramic view," demonstrating his constant concern for siting. The sizable two-story house, consisting of six bedrooms (two identified as "ser[vant] room") and three and a half baths, tantalizingly recalls the 1939 Gilboy House in its splayed wings to either side of a central living core. However, in this design, a curved entryway encloses a circular dining area before it spins off to form the living room. This striking feature is unlike anything in the Gilboy House. Hoover's architectural thinking seems to have expanded with each successive house, demonstrating a ratcheting up of his confidence and palpable excitement in exploring the possibilities of his basic conception. Then war came. Architecture had to be put on hold.

During the 1930s and 1940s, Hoover developed two alternatives to his architectural practice, first in reaction to the Great Depression that diminished the need for architecture and then to World War II right on its heels, which limited practice in "non-essential" professions. He became a part-time instructor at the Lowthorpe School of Landscape Architecture for Women and then, during the war, began working full-time as an industrial designer for Raytheon.

The Lowthorpe School of Landscape Architecture for Women in Groton, Massachusetts, had the distinction of being only the country's second professional program in landscape architecture.[1] Harvard's School of Landscape Architecture preceded Lowthorpe's formation by a year and offered a four-year degree program but was open only to men. Lowthorpe, in contrast, issued its women students a certificate for a three-year program that stressed "the idea of learning by doing, on the fact that the student, by personal experience with realities, gains permanent understanding and skill to a degree that cannot be equaled by any other method."[2]

It is possible that Lowthorpe sought to distinguish itself in this way from Harvard's more theoretically based program. Judith Eleanor Motley Low (1841–1933) founded the school in 1901. She had studied at Swanley Horticultural College, England, and had horticulture in her background; her grandparents' Boston estate,

bequeathed to Harvard University, became the Arnold Arboretum in 1872.

Hoover's association with the school probably began in the early 1930s. Perhaps Fletcher Steele steered Hoover there, since he had been closely involved with Lowthorpe as early as 1915, becoming a trustee and remaining a lecturer there until 1945.[3] Or perhaps Hoover's great friend from Harvard, Carol Fulkerson, M.A. Landscape Architecture, 1926, with whom Hoover had traveled in Europe in the 1920s, influenced his decision. Fulkerson between 1932 and 1942 taught at the Cambridge School of Domestic Architecture and Landscape Architecture, which was loosely affiliated with Lowthorpe in 1926–27.[4]

Whatever the case, according to publicity for the school, Hoover is first listed as teaching a course in "Presentation" in 1932–33.[5] A somewhat later listing of faculty, 1937–38, indicates that Hoover had provided "lectures and criticisms" over the "past two years."[6] By 1942–44 he was teaching "Design and Construction" and is shown on the catalogue cover going over a site plan with a student (Figure 4.1). Another photograph in the same publication shows him holding a "Conference in the Drafting Room" with more students.[7] One student who studied at Lowthorpe between 1943 and 1945 recalled some of the faculty: "Mr. Marquis from Olmsted Brothers who taught construction, Professor Hamblin from Harvard, who taught plant material, plus

FIGURE 4.1 Hoover working with student. Cover of Catalogue (1942–44), Lowthorpe School of Landscape Architecture and Horticulture. Groton Historical Society, Groton, MA. Courtesy of the Groton Historical Society.

one person who taught design. His name escapes me, however, I remember he was a very slight person with a mustache, and lived in his 'summer house' as he called it that he designed himself."[8]

No doubt this was Hoover. References to build and mustache, even to a "summer house," tantalizingly conjure up Hoover. He had a dry sense of humor, and the phrase amusingly evokes his own indoor-outdoor house. The same student in her memoirs went on to recall there was "no gasoline, and the moral[e] got kind of low at times" during the war.[9] Hoover in fact bicycled to Groton to teach, a trip that involved at least a ten-mile ride to Lowthorpe, assuming he left from Lincoln.

Hoover also worked during the war at Raytheon, a large electronics firm in Waltham, Massachusetts. By 1943 he was probably part of the company, perhaps even by 1942, given the fact that one of two highly technical engineering texts found in Hoover's library bears a Raytheon stamp dated 1942.[10] Whenever his family would ask what he was involved with, Hoover would reply, "I'm sorry, it's a military secret." Guessing was futile. All the family knew was that Hoover had obtained the position

through a friend. Only at war's end could he answer their question. It had to do with radar.

British radar had "made the crucial difference" to the Royal Air Force during the Battle of Britain, enabling pilots to detect nocturnal hostile movement while the enemy was blind.[11] The message to the United States, by 1942 facing defeat at sea, was clear: microwave radar was crucial to the upcoming battle for supremacy in the Atlantic and Pacific. However, Great Britain and the U.S. were unable to build the essential magnetron tubes fast enough to meet the vastly increased wartime demand for radar. The U.S. Navy, looking for sites to produce the tubes on an accelerated basis, was impressed by how relatively advanced Raytheon's SG (seagoing microwave radar) program was, while "wartime secrecy…shrouded the individual contributions of the men at Raytheon (who worked on it)."[12] By early 1943, Raytheon's initiative and concentrated effort paid off. Most of the navy's combat ships were supplied with Raytheon SG radars.[13] Subsequently, Raytheon began producing smaller radars for use on PT boats.[14]

Details of Hoover's work at Raytheon are lacking. As

an industrial designer with the radar project, he probably would have been assigned to Fritz Gross, Raytheon's chief designer on the SG project.[15] As an industrial engineer, Gross would have wanted to tap Hoover's ability to comprehend and render complex detail with amazing clarity.[16] Or, Gross would have found Hoover's architectural ability useful in aiding in the design of efficient, practicable housing for U.S. Navy SG radar installations or the SO smaller PT-boat radars.[17] Shortly after the war, Raytheon employed engineers to design "a cabinet for the magnetron with inside trays in which cold sandwiches could be heated and served."[18] Gross dedicated himself to improving the original cabinet, which leaked microwave energy. The result was the Radarange, the first commercially viable microwave oven.[19] Interestingly, Hoover's papers include carefully rendered drawings made over a decade later of what appear to be housings for "automat"-type food dispensers.

During the war, Hoover traveled back and forth, physically as well as mentally, between two very different worlds. At Lowthorpe he taught in a quiet profession at a quiet school in a quiet town; at Raytheon, Hoover worked in a culture of speed and innovation under pressure to produce critical instruments for the war. Perhaps this schizophrenic-like split in his professional life helped Hoover get through the war, utilizing as it did two interests and abilities of his, but it cannot have helped him physically. To enable him to better concentrate and to provide a calmer, certainly warmer environment (given wartime fuel rationing), his wife and children spent many months in her hometown in Georgia in 1944.

After World War II, Hoover resumed the residential practice he had begun in Lincoln. By then, he was better known within the community. As early as 1940, he had been appointed Building Inspector and in 1944 served with other Lincoln architects, including Gropius, on a committee to investigate sites for future Lincoln schools. That year he became a member of the Board of Appeals and its chair in 1949. Membership in the First Parish Church, which he had joined in 1939, also broadened his connections within the town. Lincoln's population in the early 1940s was less than two thousand; by participating in town civic institutions, it was easy for Hoover to get to know people.

Although its postwar population remained small, Lincoln was changing. Zoning laws affecting residential lot sizes had been established in 1929, but less than a decade later, in 1936, one-acre zoning went into effect, with two acres becoming the legal lot size in 1955. The Old Concord Turnpike was upgraded that same year to a modern highway, State Route 2, which facilitated commuting between Boston/Cambridge and Lincoln. In 1959, Route 128, a circumferential highway around the city of Boston just outside Lincoln's eastern boundary, was completed. All these changes increased Lincoln's accessibility and desirability while making it more expensive. Lincoln also attracted modern architects. Renowned Bauhaus architect Walter Gropius had already designed his house in Lincoln by 1938 and was soon followed by Marcel Breuer.

Among other architects attracted to postwar Lincoln were John Quincy Adams, Lawrence B. Anderson, Walter F. Bogner, Carl Koch, G. Holmes Perkins, Constantin A. Pertzoff, and Hugh Stubbins, many of whom, like Hoover, designed their own residences. Together these professionals established Lincoln as the primary locus of modern residential architecture in New England.[1]

Hoover's first postwar clients were Dr. Robert Laurent and Alice Woodward DeNormandie, prominent residents in town. Besides his medical practice, Dr. De-Normandie authored several texts in his specialty, obstetrics. His father, the Rev. James DeNormandie, had a long history in Lincoln, having become the regular minister for the Unitarian Church, later the First Parish, in 1903. For years, both generations of DeNormandies had summered in Lincoln on adjacent properties. Dr. Robert DeNormandie first built a summer home around 1910, and by 1930 he had made Lincoln his permanent home. Perhaps the growing families of the Robert De-Normandie children explain why the elder DeNormandies decided to build again. In 1946 the couple, by then in their late sixties, contacted Hoover.[2] Besides satisfying his clients, the resulting house would prove invaluable to Hoover's practice.

The DENORMANDIE HOUSE (1946–47) is located on just over two acres in Lincoln's historic center. Nearby lie the town's 1837 Arbor Vitae cemetery and Flint Fields, part of a land grant to the Flint family in the seventeenth

DENORMANDIE/NICKERSON   1947

century.[3] Treed largely with white pine and oak, the land slopes eastward down to a pond.[4] On this site, the low, flat-roofed, one-story brick house of just over 2,200 square feet is set back but visible from Lexington Road (Figure 5.1). The house's splayed rectangle plan of two wings extending primarily northeast/southwest shares many characteristics with the Gilboy House (Figure 5.2). Hoover obliquely off-centers the front entrance, but here set back at the junction of the two wings of the house. The planar entrance facade is also similarly restrained as a result of minimal fenestration and a wooden frieze running above the brick, visually elongating the house. Only a single full-height glazed panel beside the front door suggests what lies beyond.

Again, Hoover is attentive to how the house is experienced. A foyer invites access to both private and service wings while highlighting passage to the living

FIGURE 5.1 West elevation, DeNormandie House. Period photograph. Courtesy of Lincoln Town Archives, Lincoln, MA.

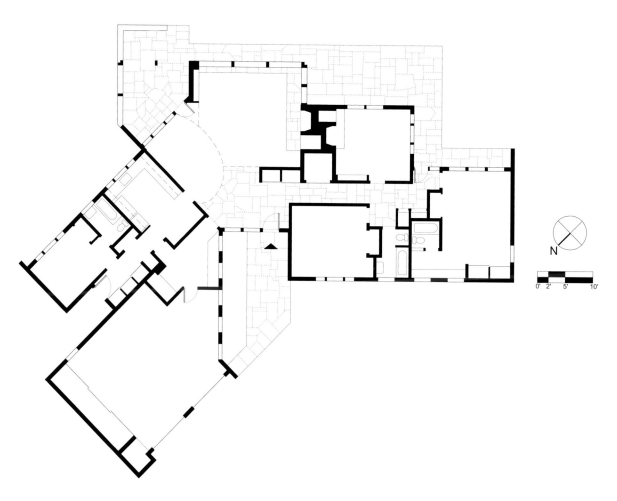

FIGURE 5.2 Plan of DeNormandie House. Drawn by Patrick Rice. HBH Papers, Hoover Family.

room ahead. Two right-angle turns dramatize arrival into that space with its long glazed wall overlooking a private pond. A brick fireplace wall opposes a bluestone paved dining area that originally led out to a similarly paved outdoor, five-sided covered terrace.[5] A curved curtain track, arcing from the kitchen to the terrace doors, allows instant redefinition of the living space according to need. Private and service spaces progress linearly northeast (kitchen, bedroom and bath, and garage) and southwest (study, two bedrooms with baths). Flooring was originally cork and asphalt, with concrete in the service area.[6]

Hoover is known to have gained new clients because of the DeNormandie House. In comparison to other modern houses, its placement relatively close to the road helped make its simple massing, warm brick facade, and distinctive blending with the landscape apparent to passersby. And to those invited inside, the house's relatively small but appealing and fluidly integrated spaces were readily appreciated. Other members of the DeNormandie family would give

Hoover commissions well into the 1980s, the last years of his practice. This body of work included another house, renovations to two more, and an ingenious composition of architectural elements saved from various parts of the demolished Spencer, Massachusetts, family home of Martha DeNormandie, wife of Robert and Alice's eldest son, James.

Between the DeNormandie House completed in 1947 and early 1949, Hoover designed four houses for Lincoln residents, located in widely dispersed areas of town.[7] In 1948 he received a commission from longtime Lincoln residents Charles and Gertrude Fitts. Fitts was an important client, a prominent Lincoln citizen. In addition to serving on several town boards, Fitts was vice president

and director of the Paine Furniture Company in Boston.[8]

The FITTS HOUSE (1948) is sited on a hilly and heavily wooded parcel, originally 14.6 acres of oak and cedar that included a deeply recessed pond, located about a mile from the center of Lincoln. Hoover took advantage of this site by setting the L-shaped house of about 2,800 square feet on and into a knoll overlooking the pond. The longer wing oriented along a north-south axis parallels Weston Road. The shorter wing, joined at a right angle along an east-west axis, follows the land's downward slope to the road to provide a basement, extended by a garage at an obtuse angle (Figure 5.3). Near the junction of the two wings, the prominent front entry composed of a projecting canopy with stone supporting wall and

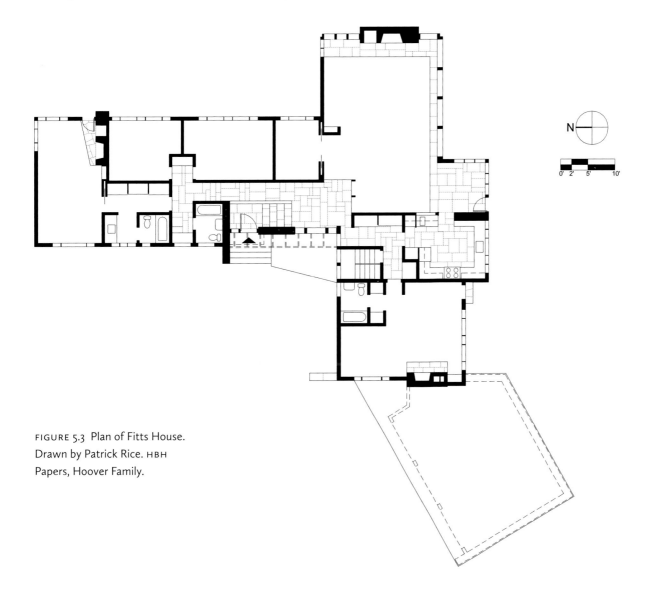

FIGURE 5.3 Plan of Fitts House. Drawn by Patrick Rice. HBH Papers, Hoover Family.

FITTS / TODD   1949

FIGURE 5.4 West elevation, Fitts
House. Period photograph.
HBH Papers, Hoover Family.

opposing thin lolly columns is approached from stone steps leading directly
from the driveway, an arrangement differing from the Gilboy's oblique or De-
Normandie's recessed doorways (Figure 5.4). On the Weston Road elevation, the
house's low gables and vertical cedar siding contrast with the forceful geome-
tries of the entry, with its front door of glazed panels within a striking fretwork
armature. Hoover's interest in fretwork will reappear numerous times in future
work and may have had its genesis in his work for Fletcher Steele.[9]

Entering the house, a right-angle turn from the foyer leads up a short flight of
stairs to a hallway. This upper landing, supporting a wooden balustrade mirroring the front door detailing provides access to both public and private wings. A
louvered screen at the end of the landing forces a left-hand turn into the public areas. From this point, a spacious, extensively glazed living/dining room projects a

full thirty feet toward the pond (Figure 5.5). A prominent fieldstone fireplace at the east end is lightened by glazed corners to either side. A library alcove to the north adds an intimate recess and contrasts with the opposing entire wall of floor-to-ceiling fixed windows to the south. In this way, Hoover maximized light and landscape and quietness in a space farthest from the road. Along the south wall and separated from the kitchen is a sunroom that utilizes a farther southern exposure. This space opens to the kitchen through that wall's "house" fretwork (Figure 5.6). Guest quarters lie behind the kitchen with basement and a two-car garage below.[10]

The private wing is to the left of the entry hallway. A long corridor leads to two bedrooms with bath and culminates in a master bedroom suite. At the ends of a secondary corridor at cross-axis are nestled opposing mini dressing areas, one serving the small bedrooms, the other the bath. Built-in cabinets surmounted by mirrors vaguely recall those in the dedicated dressing room in the Gilboy House. As in that house, the master bedroom contains a fireplace.

FIGURE 5.6 Original cabinetry separating dining room and kitchen, Fitts House. Courtesy of Joseph and Christine Ward. HBH Papers, Hoover Family.

FIGURE 5.5 Living room, Fitts House. Period photograph. HBH Papers, Hoover Family.

FIGURE 5.7 West elevation, former Pierce-Ropes House. Period photograph. Gift of the Heck Family, HBH Papers, Hoover Family.

The use of fieldstone throughout on both internal and external vertical surfaces links the interior and exterior in the living room and elsewhere: guest quarters' fireplace, entry hall, and west entry facade retaining wall. Another type of stone, flagstone, is introduced horizontally before the living room windows, for the entire sunroom through the kitchen up to the guest quarters, the hallway above the foyer to the bedrooms, and the hearth of the master bedroom suite fireplace. Floors were oak except for linoleum in the kitchen and bathrooms. Wood paneling softens the prevalence of stone. It forms a course above the stone in the entry and is used for the entry balustrade as well as the wall to the kitchen visible from the living/dining room.

The Fitts House's relative proximity to a public road made it, like the somewhat earlier DeNormandie House, a promotional mechanism for Hoover's post–World War II career. Hoover's two prewar Lincoln houses had had no such visibility. The Fitts House has further career-related importance in that it demonstrates Hoover's in-

terest in technological developments, prompted perhaps by his industrial work during the war. Hoover introduced hot-water-based copper pipe radiant heating, an innovative procedure at the time, one he would continue to use throughout most of his career.[11] Also in the public areas Hoover recessed five movable "eyeball" brass light fixtures in the ceiling cleanly without trim; unusually for the period, these were activated from possibly custom-made dimmer switchboards.[12] Along the length of the upper hallway, Hoover installed another light fixture of his own design. Triangular in section, the wooden housing sides another form of recessed lighting. And, in keeping with Hoover's lifelong engagement with landscape design, he drew up a detailed landscape plan for the Fitts property, specifying names, numbers and location of plantings, to further integrate the house with its all-important site.[13]

A commission from Stanley and Mary Higbee Heck in 1948 offered Hoover not only a different challenge but also an opportunity to make an unusually provocative statement. The Hecks asked Hoover to remodel an imposing Second-Empire house that they had purchased in 1943.[14] The Hecks, both from Burlington, Iowa, moved to Lincoln in 1940 and quickly became active in the community.[15] They resided at one time on Trapelo Road, not far from the Hoovers, so perhaps in that way came to know Hoover and chose him as their architect. The 1860–61 structure, known as the Pierce-Ropes House, was "one of Lincoln's earliest Victorian country estates" (Figure 5.7).[16] Hoover had a scheme in readiness by 1948, and on January 12, 1949, applied for permission from the town to "alter buildings" and appended a telling note to the building form in capital letters:

> This is repair work and it is impossible to tell at this time how much of the existing structure is unsound (work is to be confined to ground floor of service section—entry, kitchen, laundry, bath and servant's room). Estimate is approx $4,000 if conditions necessitate more extensive repairs are necessary I will report additional work. H.H.[17]

This work launched a far more ambitious project. When it was done, the family moved into the renovated section. Hoover went on to completely renovate the Victorian mansion.

The HECK HOUSE (1949–50), originally a three-story house of over 5,300 square feet, fronted west and was set back from a principal road leading into Lincoln center. Although the property was approximately thirteen acres at the time the Hecks bought it, the estate grew to seventeen as a result of further land purchases by the Hecks. To the east, the house overlooked historic Flint Field; mature plantings surrounded the house. With its pronounced staircase bay, mansard and dormer roofs, screened downstairs porch, and upstairs sleeping porch, the house had all the features of a Victorian country place. The house's orientation and massing seem to have inspired rather than constrained Hoover, for he maintained both the house's east/west orientation and its basically symmetrical plan, anchored by the fulcrum of the original staircase bay (Figure 5.8). However, he reinterpreted the traditional ratios of wood siding, large-paned windows, and native fieldstone by significantly increasing the amount of glass, particularly in the stair bay, and notably changing the siding from horizontal to vertical boarding. The result is of a taut yet flexible volume emphasized by the new flatness of the facade, the razor edge of the cornice, and the carefully orchestrated scale of the grids of windows and recessed doors. The problem, as he defined it, was to respect the original volume while simplifying it, bringing in more light and opening up the interior spaces to take greater advantage of the views and grounds. To this end, even as he replaced the complex roofscape with a very slightly pitched roof, he used the strong projecting cornice the length of the house to evoke the earlier, more elaborate Victorian design while effectively screening the sun from the upper sleeping rooms (Figure 5.9).

Within, Hoover affirmed the overall proportions and rectilinear footprint of the 1861 house while making significant functional and aesthetic changes. He kept the twelve-foot ceilings and formal arrangement of public rooms: entrance foyer, staircase bay with dining room behind and living room to one side. However, what had been discrete rooms were now subtly opened to yield more fluid spatial relationships. Sectioned partitions filled with fine bamboo screening integrated dining and living rooms, without interior doors to close off the downstairs spaces. The living room and the library (formerly the sun porch) shared a fireplace wall with a wide opening to one side of that wall thereby enhancing the fluidity of interior space.

Just as he opened up the interior, Hoover went to considerable lengths to erode the boundary between house and garden. Along the glazed wall of the south living room, he sunk "plant pockets" directly into stone paving that extended from fireplace to terrace between the living room and library on the garden facade. Use of vegetation to meld exterior and interior exploited a device he had

FIGURE 5.8 Plan of Heck House. Drawn by Patrick Rice. HBH Papers, Hoover Family.

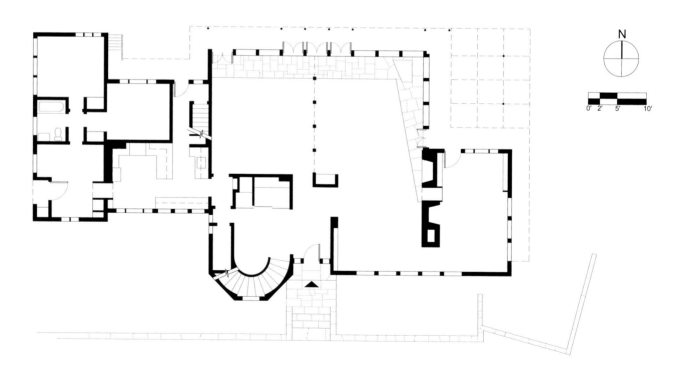

HECK   ALTERATION   1949

used more modestly in the entrance to the DeNormandie House. Furthermore, the new terrace faced away from public view to overlook the field in contrast to the street-side orientation of Victorian porches. In short, Hoover's renovations neither ignored nor simply refurbished the Pierce-Ropes House but realized a reinterpretation that yielded, as one historian has said, an "exemplary project by one of Lincoln's foremost modernist architects."[18]

Hoover's work of the 1940s marks the resurgence of his career as a residential architect. Other houses followed in the forties in rapid succession. Although differentiated by client expectations and budgets and by the variations of the sites, they are all distinguished by their flat roofs, extended expansive use of glass to take advantage of the views, and the exploitation of postwar building technologies. Although in these respects this group differs from Hoover's only two complete prewar houses, the Heck House, concluding Hoover's work of the 1940s, is superbly sui generis.

FIGURE 5.9 West elevation, Heck House. Period photograph. Courtesy of Lincoln Town Archives, Lincoln, MA.

In the 1950s, Hoover advanced certain design characteristics that he had explored in the 1940s. He continued to exploit a site's topography for residential design that generally maintained a land-hugging configuration, while occasionally incorporating a more accentuated multilevel sequence. Hoover kept the generally low profile for his houses, while exploring slightly pitched roofs to activate ceiling planes often accentuated by skylights that define and illumine interior spaces. Hoover maintained an emphasis on a plan's singular viewpoint, while introducing cross-axial vistas or atriums offering an interior landscape focus. He further worked with greater complexity of volumes through "H"-shaped floor plans and variants on hexagonal and octagonal schemes (Figure 6.1).[1] These developments led to more generous glazing, modular organization, and use of new materials, such as concrete block. Although not necessarily distinct from other architects' work of the period, Hoover's 1950s houses grew out of architectural premises important to him from the outset of his career.

This decade was Hoover's most prolific. The town of Lincoln, with a population of just under three thousand by 1955, was experiencing dramatic postwar growth. New building sites had opened up, and people had become familiar with Hoover's previous work. Hoover received forty-seven commissions for private residences, completing all but three. Despite this volume of work, he found time to respond to three nonresidential projects:

Lincoln Public Library addition, Lincoln Public School system buildings, and numerous industrial design initiatives.[2] Given this demand for his services, Hoover decided in 1955 to form a partnership with another Lincoln architect, Walter Lee Hill. This firm, which became Hoover and Hill Associates, is discussed in a subsequent chapter.

Most auspicious for Hoover was the emergence of five subdivisions in Lincoln in the 1950s substantially devoted to modern architecture.[3] Collectively, they had the effect of stimulating an appetite for that mode of architecture and changed the appearance of the town. Hoover contributed to all but two. Earlier enclaves of modernism, such as Woods End Road, laid out by Bogner in 1939, contained the work of architects within the Gropius circle.[4] But Hoover had designed two houses of the 1940s in a 1930s subdivision, Beaver Pond Road. And in the 1950s Hoover designed four houses in Old Concord Road, a subdivision established in 1940 by John Quincy Adams, and to which Adams himself contributed a number of houses. The principal modern subdivisions of that decade, however, were: Tabor Hill Road (1952) (six Hoover houses), initially comprising twelve lots; Huckleberry Hill Road (1953) (three Hoover houses), Lincoln's largest postwar subdivision with nearly thirty lots of prime land; Brown's Wood (1955), totaling twenty-three lots (two Hoover houses); and two subdivisions set out by Constantin Pertzoff, Woodcock Lane (1955) and Twin

Pond Lane (1960). Nevertheless, the first two subdivisions overlooking the Cambridge Reservoir served Hoover well.

Huckleberry Hill was the enterprise of Harold Adler, who had been chief mechanical engineer in Raytheon's radar division during the war. Possibly at that time Hoover first met Adler, and later, when Adler decided to move from Belmont, Massachusetts, it may have been Hoover who told Adler about land available in Lincoln.[5] In any case Adler offered $75,000 for a 125-acre tract of heavily wooded land near Hoover's property.[6] Its owner, Frederick H. Pollard, was delighted and accepted the deal.[7] When banks balked at loaning Adler the necessary funds, friends pitched in to help him buy the land. In 1953, he obtained approval from the town to subdivide the property into house lots, formed Stratford Realty Company, Inc., and named the new development Huckleberry Hill.[8] He first identified seven lots for sale, and as they sold, he deposited the funds in the bank, getting approval to extend the subdivision. In 1955, Adler was ready to

FIGURE 6.1 Plan for Wilkoff House.
HBH Papers, Hoover Family.

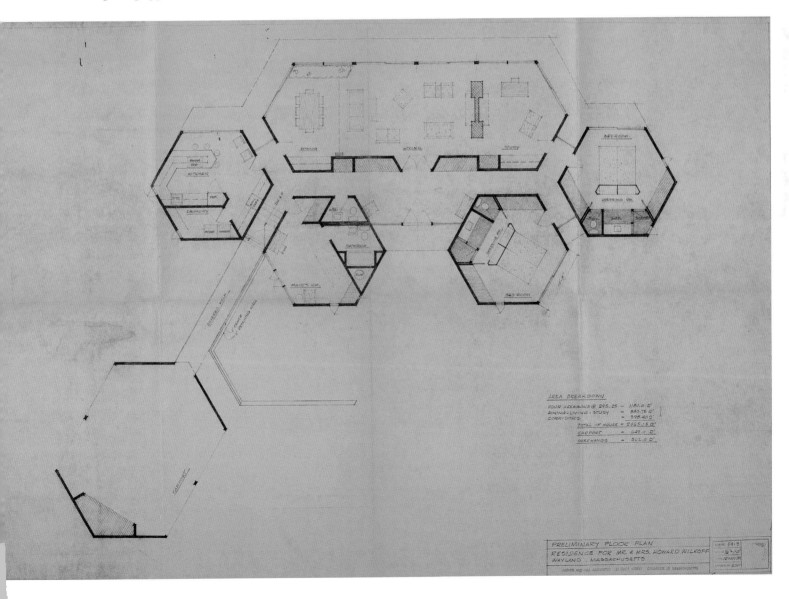

FIGURE 6.2 West elevation, Adler House. HBH Papers, Hoover Family.

build his own house there and chose Hoover to design it.[9] The house for Harold Adler and his wife, Ruth, is one of the three that Hoover designed on Huckleberry Hill, the other two being for Karl Kasparian (1954) and Thomas Witherby (1961).[10]

Adler reserved for himself the choicest lot, two and a quarter acres at the very end of Huckleberry Hill Road. The wooded hilltop drops precipitously eastward from a ledge outcropping toward the Cambridge Reservoir. The remainder of the land of oak and pine slopes gently to the west. Hoover understood the potential of this land:

> The design has been taken care of by the site. My contribution is to devise, within rather personal guidelines, a structure satisfying the mechanics of contemporary shelter. For instance, before the Adler house was built, the view was hidden by a ledge outcropping; distance and height were expected but unseen until one climbed around to the cliff side, when space seemed to burst open. It was superb.[11]

Adler apparently had some concern with the cost of an initial scheme, for Hoover wryly mentioned having "just spoiled his [Harold's] evening by giving him Tobiason's [the contractor's] bid on his house $59,995.05. I have to see him tomorrow night to discuss how we can cut the price in two without changing anything."[12] However, the size and detailing of the house as completed suggest no compromise was made after all.

The ADLER HOUSE (1955) consists of nearly 3,900 square feet. Hoover was inspired to design a house fully responsive to the precipitous site. The house, unassumingly one-story at entry level, follows the topography to become two full stories on the Reservoir side (Figure 6.2). Its unequal segments stretched along the top of the ledge meet at right angles and are slightly canted from the spine to form a modified H plan. The larger segment is specifically aligned northeast-southwest to maximize the view (Figure 6.3).

The entry opens to a generous hallway of irregular-patterned slate flooring. Indigenous ledge intrudes through the exterior wall into this space.[13] Hoover later commented, "Much of natural features [are] retained and inside and out."[14] From the hallway, windows offer a partial glimpse of the Cambridge Reservoir, prefiguring the prospect achieved after a delayed turn into the living/ dining area. This great room dramatically projects into the landscape as a virtually detached rectilinear volume. Massive floor-to-ceiling stone walls, angled left and encompassing a fireplace, dominate the room. Only then, after confronting this stonescape, does the Reservoir come fully into view, dramatically staged by the expanse of floor-to-ceiling glass on three sides of the room. This

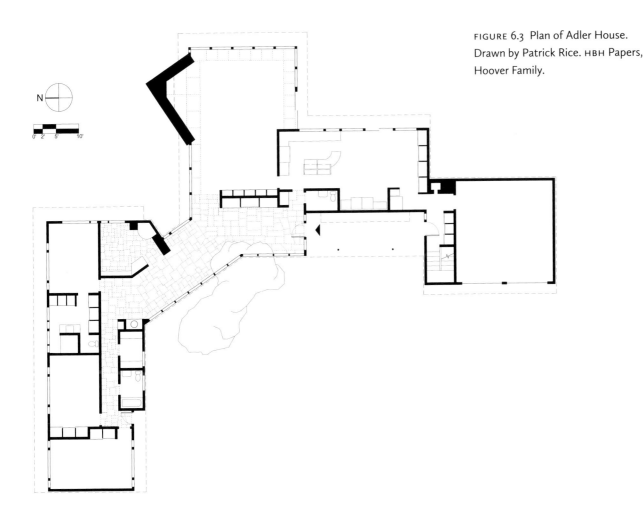

FIGURE 6.3 Plan of Adler House. Drawn by Patrick Rice. HBH Papers, Hoover Family.

N

0' 2' 5'   10'

ADLER   1955

FIGURE 6.4 South elevation, Adler House. Period photograph. Courtesy of Lincoln Town Archives, Lincoln, MA.

experiential sequence confirms Hoover's intent, as he later expressed it: "At Adlers I had wanted to preserve the impact of the suddenly expanding view" (Figure 6.4).[15] Hoover went further to design a rock garden visible only from the windows of the great room overlooking the Reservoir. Taking advantage of natural rock formations below, he created a pool mirroring the distant Reservoir and a wooden arced footbridge (Figure 6.5). Hoover's ability to merge house and site was seldom so clearly evident.

After providing entrance to the great room, the entry hallway leads left into the private wing (study, bedrooms and baths) and right into the service wing (kitchen, family room or "playroom" on the plan, utility space, and garage). The sloping land on the Reservoir side allows for a basement-level workshop, utilities, and an outdoor barbecue area. Adler dedicated this lower floor for manual work, utilizing his sizable collection of mechanical equipment, in contrast to the study on the main floor dedicated to mental work, underscored by a large blackboard on which Adler could make notations imbedded in the wall above the fireplace. Perhaps in response to his client's innovative entrepreneurship, one of the earliest floor-and-ceiling radiant heating systems was installed.[16]

Hoover would continue an architect-client relationship with Adler long after he designed Adler's house. In line with his real estate interests, Adler initiated another subdivision, Stratford Way, adjoining Huckleberry Hill. In the fall of 1979, Hoover prepared preliminary plans for this subdivision, for which he continued to explore possibilities as late as the mid-1980s.[17] When inadequate percolation made R-1 (single-family district) zoning impossible, Hoover tried to compensate with R-3 (open-space residential district) "cluster" zoning that would have left portions of land designated as open space, while incorporating the few that could perk. But Adler and the other parties involved could not come to an agreement on a proposed subdivision, and Hoover's involvement came to nothing.[18] The ultimate outcome was a different sort of development with which Hoover had nothing to do.

FIGURE 6.5 View of Cambridge Reservoir from Adler House. HBH Papers, Hoover Family.

Hoover was involved with another subdivision of the 1950s on Tabor Hill, which actually preceded Huckleberry Hill by a year. Again almost literally in Hoover's backyard, this subdivision was created from thirty wooded, sometimes ledgy acres overlooking the Cambridge Reservoir.[19] Its owner, Beatrice W. Emerson (Mrs. Edward F.) had refused earlier individual offers for some of the land, according to one of the purchasers of a parcel there.[20] But when Edgar Moor, vice president of United Shoe Machinery, and Lincoln resident and realtor Robert Pearmain approached her to purchase the entire property, she decided to sell.[21] Pearmain had met Moor soon after World War II and had already estab-

FIGURE 6.6 South elevation, Moor House. Period photograph. Courtesy of Lincoln Town Archives, Lincoln, MA.

lished a corporation, curiously named "Modern Colonial Homes."[22]

Together they acquired the land and divided the acreage into twelve large lots. Moor retained for himself five-plus acres at the end of what would become Tabor Hill Road (originally Medina Road), and soon after his marriage in 1951, hired Hoover. The Moors had been introduced to Hoover by Lincoln realtor Christopher Hurd. In 1953 Hoover designed for Moor a low, rectilinear house (demolished in 1996) that kept to the ridge, its living room projecting over the rocky promontory toward the Reservoir (Figs. 6.6, 6.7, 6.8).[23]

For the "Moor" subdivision of twelve lots, Hoover designed half of the houses. Given that Hoover's were for six different clients and not for a developer or in a subdivision established by a single architect, Hoover was instrumental in shaping the predominately modern character of this subdivision.[24] Land prices at Tabor Hill were evidently modest enough to attract forward-minded

professionals with MIT or Harvard connections and others interested in innovative architecture. Receptive to new ideas, they sought Hoover out for commissions between 1953 and 1956. His clients, in addition to Moor, were Stephen Crandall (house initially built by Crandall 1953, substantial additions by Hoover 1960–61); Leopold Peavy (house 1954–55); James Faran (house 1954–55); Charles Satterfield (house 1955); and Richard Bolt (house initiated by Bolt after 1954, Hoover 1957).[25]

The second house on the "hill" by Hoover with a Reservoir overlook was commissioned by Leopold Peavy, Jr., an investment banker with Estabrook & Co., later vice president of Tucker Anthony, Inc. The link between Peavy, Hoover, and Tabor Hill was again Lincoln realtor Christopher Hurd, who advised Peavy that land was available.[26] Peavy's awareness of Hoover may have also come from his friendship with Charles Fitts, whose house Hoover designed in 1948. Peavy purchased for $8,000 a lot of over four and a half acres that offered a

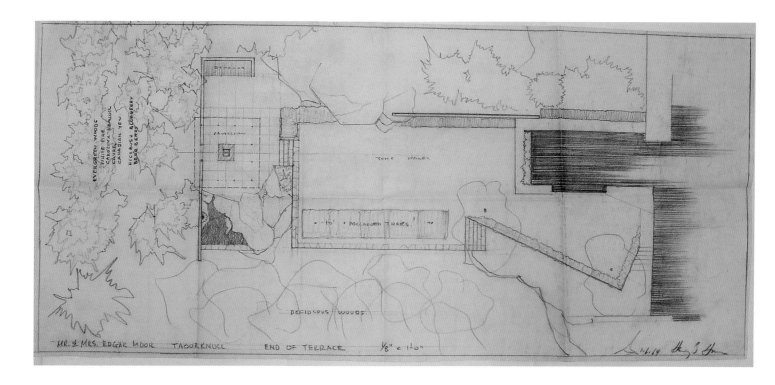

FIGURE 6.7 Terrace, Moor House. Drawn by Hoover. HBH Papers, Hoover Family.

wide view of the Cambridge Reservoir from the vantage point of a high ledge. There being no road to the site at time of purchase, Leo and his new wife, Elizabeth Johnson Peavy, had to walk through the woods to their land.

The Peavys were uncertain as to exactly what they wanted in a house, but they loved modern architecture. Elizabeth grew up in Wisconsin admiring the work of Frank Lloyd Wright, recalling that most of her friends had lived in Wright houses. The Peavys admired Hoover's houses because they were "simple" (unpretentious), inside and out. Elizabeth Peavy specifically mentioned Hoover's penchant for "built-in 'things.'" "Hoover told us exactly what we wanted!"

Hoover's scheme for the PEAVY HOUSE (1954–55) took inspiration from the site's steep outcropping. Sensitive to that feature, Hoover at dinner with the Peavys in Boston before construction began suddenly flipped the plan, sensing that stepping down to a living room was better than to bedrooms. The approximately 4,000-square-foot one-story, flat-roofed house (storage area below) was sensitive to the ridgeline along a north-east/south-west axis. In plan, the house consisted of a central rectangular core with two splayed wings (Figure 6.9). Hoover's slightly recessed entrance at the juncture of these wings recalled in more amplified form the postwar plans of the DeNormandie and Fitts houses of the late 1940s.[27]

MR. EDGAR MOOR
TABOR KNOLL – END OF TERRACE   ⅛"=1'0"

FIGURE 6.8 Pavilion, Moor House.
Drawn by Hoover. HBH Papers,
Hoover Family.

Upon approach, an oblique sightline through the glazed entrance dramatically clarified the rationale for house's siting: the Reservoir beyond (Figure 6.10). Once inside the glazed entry hallway, a right turn revealed a full view of the Reservoir from an outdoor terrace with pergola, a view again visible at the living room at the far end of the hallway. The Reservoir side of the living room was fully glazed, floor to ceiling (Figure 6.11). The hallway also gave access to the dining room and kitchen with maid's room and bath and two-car garage beyond forming a service wing splayed from the main block of the house. Opposing this wing on the other side of the entrance was another splayed wing for private use containing three bedrooms with two baths and playroom. The owners' private spaces extended at right angles to the entry hallway: study at hallway level; and then up two steps, master suite with dressing room and bath. This suite ended in a small balcony

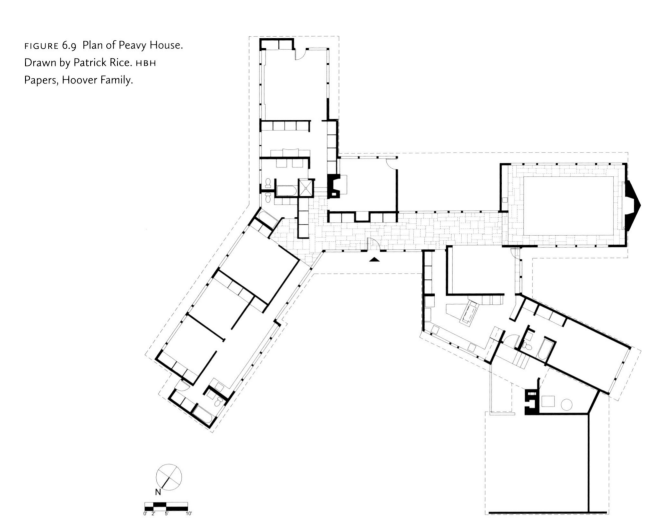

FIGURE 6.9 Plan of Peavy House.
Drawn by Patrick Rice. HBH
Papers, Hoover Family.

N
0 2'   5'   10'

projected toward the Reservoir, as had the Moor living room of the year before (Figure 6.12).

Hoover characteristically paid close attention to materials and their application. He used ⅜-inch plate glass throughout to avoid fogging problems common with thermopane glass of the 1950s. Flagstone was designated for the entry hallway, a three-foot edging of the living room floor and one side of the dining room. Hoover, appreciating its warm pinkish tone, employed Tennessee crab-orchard stone for the study and living room fireplaces. Asphalt tile appeared in the kitchen, maid's room, and children's wing, but cork flooring, because of its noise-deafening property, was used in the dining room, study, and master bedroom. Although intended also for the living room, it was not laid because a contractor mistake in pouring the concrete bed made the floor too high to accommodate the cork; wall-to-wall carpeting was chosen instead. Hoover selected Philippine mahogany for interior paneling in the dining room, designing all the cabinets and cupboards.[28] Elsewhere, Hoover specified Novoply sliding doors, a product of the 1950s.[29] Radiant heating was installed in both floor (iron pipes) and ceiling (copper).

The Peavy House was Hoover's largest to date. For the

FIGURE 6.10 Northwest elevation, Peavy House. HBH Papers, Hoover Family.

FIGURE 6.11 Southeast elevation, Peavy House. HBH Papers, Hoover Family.

FIGURE 6.12 Southeast elevation with master bedroom wing, Peavy House. HBH Papers, Hoover Family.

1950s, it would not likely have been considered a "modest" house. It is considerably larger today. Even so, despite extensive modifications by two successive owners, in 2004 and 2013, the house's basic, though amplified, footprint and appearance of having grown from its unique landscape, remain intact.[30]

A third Tabor Hill house by Hoover was for Charles N. Satterfield, MIT professor of chemical engineering, and his wife, Anne, who met fellow MIT professor Stephen Crandall and his wife, Patricia, while living in Cambridge. At MIT Anne and Patricia attended a course on "Small Dwelling Construction" taught by professor of civil and environmental engineering Albert G. H. Dietz, which probably propelled them to decide to build houses of their own.[31] Doing so was, as Satterfield put it, "a popular idea after the war." The Satterfields began looking in Lincoln, learned of Hoover and commissioned him to design a modern house with simple lines and "no fancy ornamentation," even before they had acquired any property. Their two-acre plot, which lies at the upper end of Tabor Hill Road, was carved out of four acres that Pearmain had purchased from Farrington Memorial bordering Tabor Hill to add to the subdivision.[32]

The SATTERFIELD HOUSE (1956–57) is a two-level, roughly 2,800-square-foot purely rectilinear house without extensions or wings. To relieve its simplicity and linearity, Hoover introduced an asymmetrical gabled roof that projects strongly beyond the entrance facade; a flat roof had been originally conceived (Figure 6.13).[33] The immediate effect is of an umbrella sheltering a lightweight screen of wood and glass panels, but in fact Hoover runs the gable transversely across the house to contour the rooms beneath. The bent axis crossing the slate foyer delays navigation into the expansive living area, made more so by the unexpected highest pitch of the ceiling occurring soon after entry. Here, the spine of the ceiling establishes an east/west axis. Set virtually at the ridgeline, two large square skylights create deep light wells from which light floods to define a seating alcove below (Figure 6.14). According to one appreciative subsequent owner, even moonlight is given "perfect entry," thereby providing "an opportunity in February and March to read by the fireplace without Edison's invention."[34] The skylights and opposing fireplace and hearth block, made intimate by the pitch of the roof and the block's opacity, form a secondary axis running north/south.[35] The living room's prevailing east/west axis is reestablished by the gentle slope of the ceiling plane toward the long north-facing glazed wall with clerestory. This configuration flattens the landscape and sense of recession; certainly the downward slope of the ceiling has the effect of concentrating the view.[36] A family room/kitchen and "three-season" screened porch to the east share that outlook.

Hoover seems to have thought of the house in modular terms (Figure 6.15). The space that includes the living/dining area and porch is marked out on the plans in "equal" 4-foot 8-inch parts. The openings, whether glazed or screened, conform to the module as does the dimension of the public area: three times for the length of the entry hall, six times for the length of the living room; and again three times for the length and width of the family room. The fixed windows in the bedrooms that extend northward from the living room, though not the room dimensions themselves, also follow this 4-foot 8-inch module.

In the Satterfield House, as in his earlier residences, Hoover established areas for specific activity within a larger open volume. Here, as described, the ceilingscape plays a much more active dramatic role in defining usage and fostering sensibility to space than in the past. Furthermore, he used a cement block wall filled with sand for soundproofing to separate the private and public areas of the house. Satterfield described it as a "70-decibel wall." The house's utilities, along with originally unfinished living space, are also separated from the rest of the house on a lower level, made possible by the land's topography.[37]

Hoover seems to have been exploring more small-scale ways to define these spaces. Built-in seating banks at right angles to a console in the living area increase the sense of floor area in this relatively small house. Several sketches on yellow tissue paper show Hoover's investigations of furniture placement in the living room and kitchen spaces to similar effect.[38] However, Hoover seems not so much set on the furniture itself as on testing its role in the house as a mise-en-scene for modern living. A broad wood slider that can be opened and closed between living/dining room and the family room permits spatial flexibility. Another sort of living arrangement Hoover designed to increase perception of interior spaciousness is an expanse of decking on the exterior beyond the family room and kitchen surrounding a small exterior garden.

In close succession to the Satterfield House, Hoover took on new clients, Alvin Schmertzler, a construction engineer, and his wife, Barbara (later Mrs. Louis Osborne). Both had admired Hoover's work from seeing his houses in Lincoln. Barbara, a graduate of the Boston

SATTERFIELD   1956

FIGURE 6.13 (*above*) South
elevation, Satterfield House. Period
photograph. Courtesy of Lincoln
Town Archives, Lincoln, MA.

FIGURE 6.14 (*left*) Living room,
Satterfield House. HBH Papers,
Hoover Family.

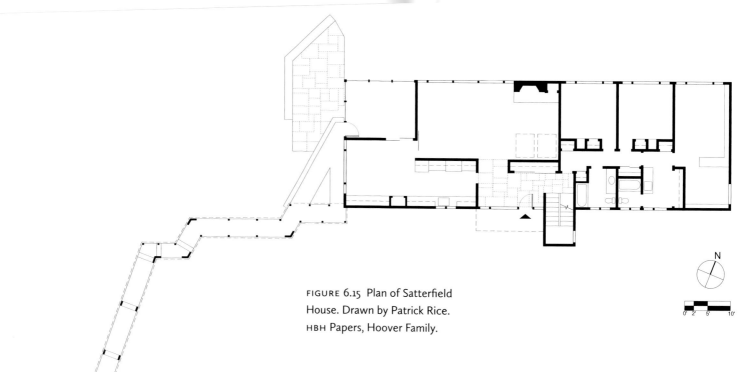

FIGURE 6.15 Plan of Satterfield
House. Drawn by Patrick Rice.
HBH Papers, Hoover Family.

Museum School, believed that good design need not cost more than pedestrian
work and sought it in a house for themselves and their two young children.[39]
The Schmertzlers had earlier engaged Hoover to design a house for them in
Auburndale, Massachusetts, but complications made building impossible.[40] The
Schmertzlers then bought a small plot of less than an acre with second-growth
trees and a stream running to the south in neighboring Lexington, Massachusetts. This land was part of a forty-two acre parcel being developed in 1952 for
modern houses by MIT-trained architects Walter Pierce and Danforth Compton.
Of the more than fifty houses built in this development called Peacock Farm,
all but four were by Compton + Pierce, and of these four, only one was completely by Hoover.[41] Compton + Pierce's approach was to use one basic model
to make their development "available to those with limited budgets in a period
when virtually all modern houses were custom designed by architects."[42] The
so-called Compton + Pierce "Peacock Farm House" had split-level facades and
an unbroken, rectilinear footprint that "could be flipped and turned to fit the
contours of the sites."[43]

The SCHMERTZLER-OSBORNE HOUSE (1957–58, 1964, 1974) is, not surpris-
ingly, a different "Peacock Farm House." Hoover specifically tailored his design
to the Schmertzlers' needs and to the individual parcel of land. The house is
basically H-shaped in plan (Figure 6.16). Hoover centered the entry under an
overhang spanning both ends of the house. The house's crossbar is a wide,
high-ceilinged volume under a slightly pitched roof with its ridgeline running
north/south. This volume contains the entry foyer, the living area with fireplace

wall, a dining area, and the kitchen, all of which are laid out in open sequence around a large atrium. Natural light from its skylight allows large plants to grow (Figure 6.17). Hoover amplified the light emanating from the atrium with floor-to-ceiling windows on the south wall and clerestory windows on the north.[44] The kitchen to the west, running the entire width of the central volume, is set off by a wall of storage cabinets not fully ceiling height. Barbara had told Hoover that she wanted a single, unbroken work surface in her kitchen, which Hoover provided in the form of one long functional work island paralleling the line of the cabinets. Beyond the kitchen, one end of which is marked "playroom" on the plans, are two children's bedrooms with laundry and bath between. To the east, on the other side of the H are master bedroom, walk-through closet, dressing room, and bath. All private areas are given greater intimacy by the lowered ceiling created by the east-west slope of the roof.

As in the Satterfield House, internal sense of order and balance is generated by the use of a module, in this case

a 6-foot 4-inch scheme, indicated on the plan along the sheet's north and south edge.[45] The module determines placement of the atrium, glazed door openings to the south, entry doorway jambs, north clerestory placements, as well as length and width of the atrium, kitchen cabinet wall and kitchen counter. Hoover also used the module to locate and inform dimensions of the fireplace surround and atrium.[46] Spatially, the central volume is six modules in length and four in width. Thus the living room area, encompassing three modules, equals the size of the dining, kitchen, and foyer areas combined. The atrium, itself a space demarked only by lightweight framing, does not interrupt visually but reinforces a sense of spaciousness. The result is a house with multiple zones, whose hierarchical relations are defined by the modular arrangement as well as by changes in both ceiling height and light. As in the Satterfield House, Hoover used all three mechanisms.

In 1974 Hoover extended the original central volume northward by adding a study to accommodate the Os-

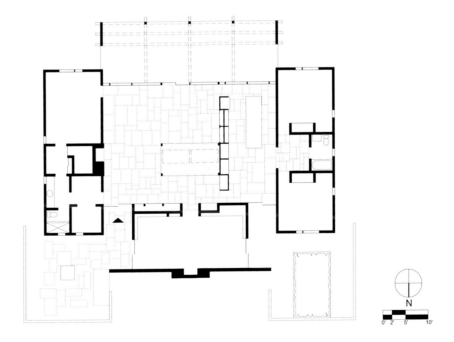

FIGURE 6.16 Plan of Schmertzler/ Osborne House. Drawn by Patrick Rice. HBH Papers, Hoover Family.

FIGURE 6.17 (*left*) Living/dining area, Schmertzler/Osborne House. HBH Papers, Hoover Family.

FIGURE 6.18 (*right*) North elevation, Schmertzler/Osborne House. HBH Papers, Hoover Family.

bornes' library and a pair of antique Japanese screens Barbara had acquired several years before.[47] The house now totaled 2,280 square feet. In the new construction the original entrance was moved slightly eastward to accommodate double wooden doors opening into the study (Figure 6.18). Clerestory windows on the north above a fireplace and full-height glass sliders at east/west corners light this new space. In 1985 Hoover added a pergola to the south, along with expanded wood decking.

The Schmertzler-Osborne House demonstrates Hoover's ability to respond to a site that was not inherently distinctive. To compensate for a lack of distant views, he shifted the drama to the interior. Furthermore, the house's low profile and planar exterior allow little of the interior to be anticipated, so that upon entering, awareness of finely detailed and elegantly conceived proportions; feeling of warmth from untreated vertical western red cedar siding, fir ceiling and supporting beams, bluestone paving; and sense of generous spatial continuity, are all the more pleasurable.[48] To accentuate the interior further, in contrast to the DeNormandie and Heck houses, in which Hoover had used planting at the rooms' perimeter to mediate with the landscape, here he offered an alternative, a pocket of nature fully within, in keeping with the scale and quietness of the modest stream and small trees outside. Hoover himself recognized this house's "very simple plan / good spacial [*sic*] qualities," observing the "recent addition [1974] perhaps successfull [*sic*] but changed character."[49] Barbara Osborne herself considered the house "a remarkable piece of design because it is, in my view, beautiful, but having inhabited it, it is also very practical."[50]

In addition to houses for clients in Lincoln and nearby Lexington, Hoover designed eleven houses between 1952 and 1964 in the town of Weston. One of those was the house Kenneth and Polly Selzer Germeshausen asked Hoover to design in 1958. It became the house the Germeshausens lived in for the rest of their lives. In seeking an architect, they had looked at many houses in the suburbs, including one that, Polly Germeshausen later recollected, "had a tree right in the middle of it."[51] That phrase clearly describes the Schmertzler/Osborne residence designed for a constrained, flat site. The Germeshausens purchased approximately thirty acres of topographically varied land in Weston and requested an altogether different sort of interior feature, a pool.

Hoover's careful investigation of the site and deliberations over design for the GERMESHAUSEN HOUSE (1958–60) matched the scientific methods of his client[52] (Figure 6.19). Germeshausen was a nuclear scientist, MIT-trained, and founder of the well-known technology company EG&G (Edgerton, Germeshausen and Grier). Germeshausen held more than fifty patents, and in 1990, the year of his death, was awarded the first annual award for technical achievement by the U.S. Defense Department, known as the Germeshausen Award.

Sketches from 1957 exist showing Hoover's consideration of various ways of utilizing the site's key topographical feature, a steep ledge outcropping. An irregularly shaped pool also appears in these sketches, making it clear that this requirement was in Hoover's mind from the start. In the final scheme, Hoover layered the house of over 2,600 square feet against the outcropping in three levels beginning at the lowest, the driveway level (Figure 6.20). From this point, Hoover makes one of the more dramatic statements of his career, running a section of roofline nearly fifty feet upward from the carport to the highest point

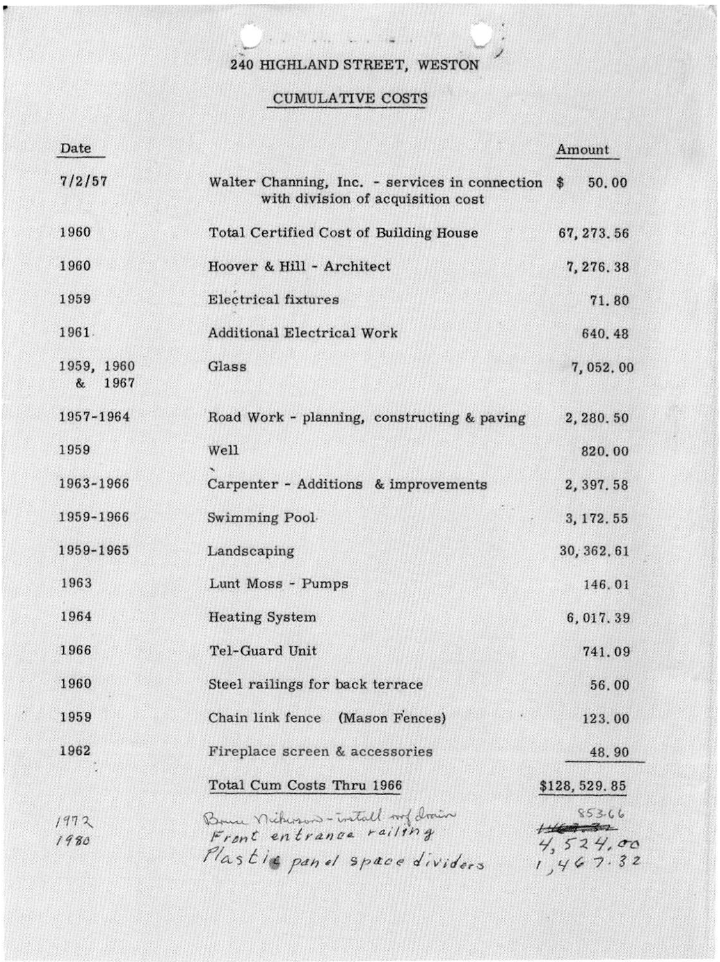

FIGURE 6.19 Receipt detailing construction expenses. Courtesy of Ann Wiedie and Keith Hartt.

240 HIGHLAND STREET, WESTON

CUMULATIVE COSTS

Date		Amount
7/2/57	Walter Channing, Inc. - services in connection with division of acquisition cost	$ 50.00
1960	Total Certified Cost of Building House	67,273.56
1960	Hoover & Hill - Architect	7,276.38
1959	Electrical fixtures	71.80
1961	Additional Electrical Work	640.48
1959, 1960 & 1967	Glass	7,052.00
1957-1964	Road Work - planning, constructing & paving	2,280.50
1959	Well	820.00
1963-1966	Carpenter - Additions & improvements	2,397.58
1959-1966	Swimming Pool	3,172.55
1959-1965	Landscaping	30,362.61
1963	Lunt Moss - Pumps	146.01
1964	Heating System	6,017.39
1966	Tel-Guard Unit	741.09
1960	Steel railings for back terrace	56.00
1959	Chain link fence (Mason Fences)	123.00
1962	Fireplace screen & accessories	48.90
	Total Cum Costs Thru 1966	$128,529.85
1972	Bruce Nickerson - install roof drain	853.66
1980	Front entrance railing	4,524.00
	Plastic panel space dividers	1,467.32

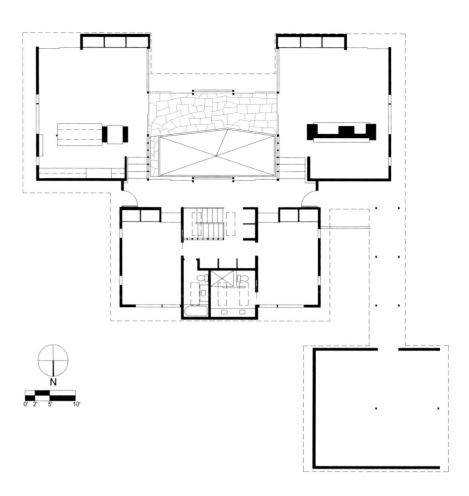

of the house, and three feet beyond.[53] The entire house progresses inexorably upward. Its entrance, reached by several broad steps, is quietly positioned in the center of this front elevation (Figure 6.21).

From the entry at the middle level, a hallway runs the full length of the house. This hallway divides public from private areas as well as demarcating middle from upper level. On the upper level are living room and study on one side, and on the other kitchen and family room, both "pavilions" reached by three steps from the hallway. These pavilions flank a large rectangular space that originally encompassed an indoor pool (Figure 6.22). The main floor's lateral and longitudinal symmetry, evident in Hoover's plan, is satisfyingly perceived when mov-

ing through the house, not as an imposed "static formal strategy" but as an organizational idea that provides a subtle but inevitable rationale for spatial placement.[54]

The trapezium-shaped pool, the house's central feature in many ways, measured twenty-two feet in length, five feet at its widest point, and approximately five feet in depth. A section of stone paving between the pool and the exterior glazed wall permitted some movement between the two public areas and provided room for houseplants to echo nature outside. Glass sliders closed off the pool at either end along the hallway side.

The Germeshausens had specifically requested an indoor environment equivalent in New England to what they had loved when visiting Hawaii: warm water and

FIGURE 6.21 (*left*) West elevation, Germeshausen House. HBH Papers, Hoover Family.

FIGURE 6.22 (*below*) Interior of Germeshausen House. Courtesy of Katherine Mierzwa.

FIGURE 6.23 View from west elevation though interior of Germeshausen House. Courtesy of Molly Bedell.

tropical plants. Hoover brilliantly made that possible by situating not a tree in the middle of the house, as he had in Lexington, but water. Polly Germeshausen also had wanted to be able to see the pool from her bedroom on the middle level. In response, Hoover gave her visual access through louvered windows. For purposes of symmetry, he repeated this access from the second bedroom. On the level below are additional bedrooms with bath and a utility space giving access to the outdoors and the carport.

The house's focus served the Germeshausens well, but the pool was probably difficult to maintain. The subsequent owners covered the pool with stone flooring, deciding to use the space for family living. They commented:

> It's interesting, how some interpretations of the house center on the pool. Perhaps I'm biased as we decided to cover the pool, but I think the house has many more amazing features: the siting, the exposure, the symmetry, the aesthetics of the finishes, etc.[55]

How right they are. It is to Hoover's credit that this house, so closely aligned to the Germeshausens' desires, could so readily be adapted to its new (second) owners' lifestyle. Hoover's "aesthetics" of materials (fir tongue-and-groove siding inside and out with redwood exterior trim, stone from the property for the living room and family room fireplaces, large expanses of glass) and Hoover's skill in integrating the house with the site (long sloping roofline extending from carport to upper level), cause the house to nestle easily against terraced gardens. Integration of inside and outside is complete (Figure 6.23).

Along with his other multiple commissions in Lincoln, Hoover began a house in Jaffrey, New Hampshire.[56] The SHEARER HOUSE (1955–57) was commissioned by William Leonard Shearer III, president of Paine Furniture Company of Boston.[57] Shearer knew two Hoover clients in Lincoln, James DeNormandie, a former classmate at Harvard, and Charles Fitts, a company vice president, for whom Hoover had designed a house in 1948. DeNormandie's parents lived in the Hoover house of 1947, previously discussed. Shearer and his wife, Constance, as frequent dinner guests, had admired their hosts' "simple and nice" house.[58] They wanted their own. At over 8,000 square feet, it would be Hoover's largest and most exuberant.[59] Although Jaffrey was relatively far from Boston and Shearer's place of work, the couple lived in the house Hoover designed for nearly fourteen years.

Shearer had hoped to build earlier, but the Korean War had prevented construction. It was not until the war's end, having purchased a spectacular piece of New Hampshire property, that Shearer hired Hoover. A busy professional, Shearer designated his wife as the main conduit to the architect. The two worked well together. Had Shearer been more actively involved with the architect, the resulting design might have been more conservative, at least on the basis of the furniture his company manufactured.[60]

Unlike the sites of Hoover's houses in Lincoln, notable for their pastoral scenes of ledges, ponds, and wooded hills, the Shearer property was truly remarkable, commanding a view of 3,166-foot Mount Monadnock and a 360-degree panorama of the lower mountains and fields below. Surrounded by conservation land, the previously farmed property retained its rural character. An old lane winding half a mile from the road to the crown of the hill became the driveway. Hoover oriented the house east/west on the highest point of the property to exploit proximity to the mountain.

The house appears from the entry as two stories but is actually Hoover's only three-story design, a grouping of three flat-roofed, interlocking stone-sided volumes stacked at right angles to each other (Figure 6.24).[61] Open and enclosed balconies projecting beyond the lower volume on three sides, with eaves supported by stone fin walls, give the uppermost floor the effect of a penthouse. The result is a luxurious sequence of flat forms to stage the weekend

FIGURE 6.24 Southeast elevation, Shearer House. HBH Papers, Hoover Family. All Shearer House photographs courtesy of Paul Giese.

parties the Shearers enjoyed on this spectacular site (Figure 6.25).

Although this house is again basically an H-plan, here the outer sections of the H are given primary emphasis (Figure 6.26). On approach to the house, the main entrance is hidden by the high granite wall of the garage until full arrival. The entrance foyer too gives no hint of theatricality beyond. Only after one of Hoover's signature right-angle turns does the spatial drama begin to unfold. A spiral staircase of Hoover's design, encased within a granite cylinder, circling upward to the master-bedroom suite, is immediately confronted (Figure 6.27). Moving forward, the landing becomes a platform ("Hall" on the plans), orchestrating passage through space. This platform effectively stages circulation into and through the principal parts of the house.

A choice is now offered: entering the dining area to the

west or descending three broad steps to a glazed hallway from which a stony meadow landscape can be viewed. From the hallway, the living room is initially obscured from view by a free-standing storage wall of Douglas fir. Not until turning left and moving beyond this wall does the size and grandeur of this room become apparent. It extends nearly thirty-five feet beyond the dining room to the fully glazed south wall (Figure 6.28). Along the west wall, a prominent granite and marble fireplace defines a seating area (Figure 6.29). The sheer breadth of this generous volume, and indeed the entire main floor, is accentuated by the uniform tonality of materials and fluid gradations in light and levels. To all appearances the house is simply one great room for dining, conversing, and circulating. But in fact, to the east on the same floor and below, are bedrooms with their own balconies or access to the terrace with swimming pool, game room

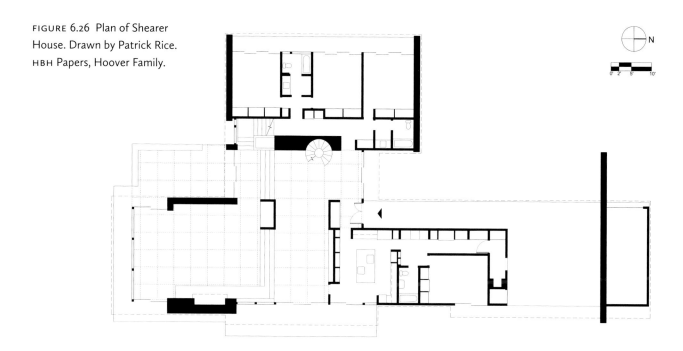

FIGURE 6.26 Plan of Shearer House. Drawn by Patrick Rice. HBH Papers, Hoover Family.

between. To the north on the main level are kitchen, bedroom, utilities, and garage.

Once again, Hoover employs modularization as a design tool to enhance perception of space. Setting a module of 6-feet 6-inches at the very entry of the house, Hoover continued to use it to inform many interior dimensions: the length of the entrance ("Threshold" on the plans) into the Hall (one module), the width of the platform steps (two modules), the width of the dining area (three modules), as well as that of the living great room at the widest point from lower platform entry to the fireplace wall opposite (four modules). It appears that even the full width of both service and bedroom wings conforms (three modules).

But perhaps what is most remarkable is the house's orientation. The great bank of windows in the living area faces south, but the mountain lies to the west beyond the window wall of the dining area (Figure 6.30). Its landmark silhouette is not even immediately visible

from the upper platform. And only after approaching the window, walking around the dining room table, or moving up from the living room area can the top of the mountain be seen. Even from the upper floor, reached from the entry platform, the view of Mount Monadnock is fully seen when looking sideways from the bed in the master bedroom or standing before the glazed wall. Confronted with the most dramatic landscape of his career, Hoover chose to make of Mount Monadnock a guest. Instead of being predictably present or easily achieved, the site must be sought. It is not delivered.[62]

The Shearer House in fact demonstrates varied ways architecture can stage an experience of landscape. Sometimes Hoover provides enough foreground to create a perspective recession. Sometimes the foreground is eliminated so the landscape appears close, flattened against the glass, but never does he give a 360-degree panorama that would allow the full extent of what might be seen to be grasped. Only the balconies give unmedi-

FIGURE 6.27 Staircase in entry hall, Shearer House. HBH Papers, Hoover Family.

ated views of the landscape. The cantilevered balcony wrapping the great room and dining area on two sides projects directly out to meadows and trees, and steps lead down from the terrace to the swimming pool at ground level.[63] Landscape is observed unfiltered as well as from the long balcony on the uppermost floor framed by the end fin walls.

Constance Shearer remarked, "You can't compete with nature. The pictures outside our windows change every season."[64] Hoover, as always, understood that. But if he couldn't compete, he would determine how nature was seen. Rather, he designed a house that may be described as a highly refined instrument for enjoying and considering the landscape. He rarely enjoyed such a combination of inimitable landscape, sympathetic and sensitive client, and unlimited resources.[65] Of the more than one hundred residential designs spanning a half-century, the Shearer House is Hoover's most dramatic achievement.[66]

In the very last year of the decade Hoover designed the MACLAURIN HOUSE (1960–61) for Elfriede, wife of MIT economics professor W. Rupert Maclaurin. Her husband had known architect Carl Koch when both were at MIT, and together they conceived the modern residential community, Conantum, Concord, Massachusetts, in the early 1950s.[67] Although Koch had designed at least two houses in Lincoln, his focus was not residential architecture. Since 1947 the couple had resided in Lincoln. A year after her husband's death in 1959, Elfriede Maclaurin acquired from her sister-in-law nine acres on Page Road and two on Page Farm

FIGURE 6.29 (*left*) Living room, Shearer House. HBH Papers, Hoover Family.

FIGURE 6.30 (*right*) View of Mt. Monadnock from dining room, Shearer House. HBH Papers, Hoover Family.

FIGURE 6.31 South elevation,
Maclaurin House. HBH Papers,
Hoover Family.

FIGURE 6.32 East elevation,
Maclaurin House. HBH
Papers, Hoover Family.

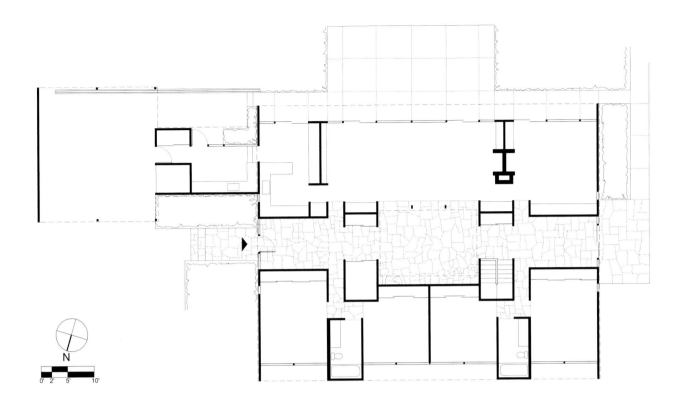

N

0' 2' 5' 10'

FIGURE 6.33 Plan of Maclaurin House. Drawn by Patrick Rice. HBH Hoover Papers, Hoover Family.

Road. For this property, she selected Hoover as her architect. No doubt she had seen Hoover's houses on Old Concord Road. But, also, according to the family, Hoover "learned what she did and did not like in her colonial house on Trapelo Road. . . . Mrs. Maclaurin raved that Henry Hoover had built exactly the house she envisioned. She loved it (as do we)."[68]

Hoover sited the Maclaurin House (1960–61) along an east-west axis on a gently contoured, lightly wooded lot bordering a meadow (Figure 6.31).[69] Its shallow-pitched roof and gabled ends cover a rectangle of nearly 2,500 square feet (Figure 6.32). The original scheme, on a plan inscribed "proposal," took the form of an H with the crossbar a completely glazed entry hall joining two rectangular segments (Figure 6.33).[70] Hoover had used this glazed-crossbar scheme in two earlier houses, Leopold Peavy (1955, Lincoln, Massachusetts) and Arthur Nelson (1958, Weston, Massachusetts). For Maclaurin, however, he reconfigured the crossbar, rotating it 90 degrees in the final scheme, so that the "hallway" is parallel to and sandwiched between the two main segments of the H. Running the full depth of the house, this space creates a light-filled core (Figure 6.34). Hoover raised and sharpened the pitch of the roof directly over the space, adding glass along the ridgeline as well as at both gabled ends. Following a modularly

FIGURE 6.34 Entry hall, Maclaurin House. HBH Papers, Hoover Family.

conceived scheme of 6-feet 2¾-inches, the two north bedrooms (two modules wide) are balanced across the atrium by a fully glazed living/dining area (approximately three modules long) and flanking kitchen and library (two modules wide). Hoover's 1960 plan shown here differs from the house built in 1961 in that Hoover moved the fireplace wall westward, thereby enlarging the living/dining area and conforming to the module. Other less substantive changes also occurred.[71]

The overall effect is startlingly like that of a Roman villa, described architecturally as "a single-storey family domus—an inward-looking, cool, and quiet house tightly organized around a core space called the atrium. . . . Usually sky-lit, with a corresponding catch basin sunk in the pavement and hooked up to a cistern below, this central room . . . [along an] axis of alternately light and dark spaces was flanked by symmetrically arranged rooms."[72] In fact, on one of his schemes Hoover included what appears to be a rectangular pool in the center of Hoover's "atrium," a feature omitted from the house as built.

Without slavishly following this model, if indeed he had one in mind, Hoover conceived the light-filled central atrium/hall as the physical and social focal point of the house. And like the Roman villa, in Hoover's linear conception, nature can be experienced not only overhead but also at the ends, where the glazed walls give a view of the outside. If "bringing of nature indoors" was another feature of Roman domestic architecture, the use of bluestone and wood flooring, vertical pickled oak siding, concrete block, and extensive use of glass, thrust this "roman" house squarely into the twentieth century.[73] It is tempting to think that here Hoover partnered his classroom and travel scholarship with his practice of modernism.[74] Later, with typical understatement, Hoover declared the house to have "Good spaces / well detailed," a statement that sums up work of the entire decade.[75]

In the decade of the fifties, after many years of private residential architectural practice, Hoover established a partnership with fellow Lincoln architect Walter Lee Hill (1924–2005).[1] Hoover's reason for this change was undoubtedly the press of commissions. Between 1947, the resumption of Hoover's career after the war, and 1955, the start of Hoover's partnership with Hill, Hoover had designed twenty-one houses in Lincoln as well as nine houses outside Lincoln.[2] Hoover clearly had too much to do with only the occasional in-house draftsman.[3] Although he had considered forming an association even earlier, not until 1955 did Hoover go into partnership as Hoover and Hill Associates.[4]

His partner Walter Hill was born in Cambridge, Massachusetts, and received a bachelor of architecture degree from the Massachusetts Institute of Technology in 1950.[5] During Hill's time at MIT, Lawrence B. Anderson and Jose Luis Sert were on the architectural faculty.[6] Anderson had designed two modern houses in Lincoln in 1950. Hill's own architectural interests leaned toward the nonresidential. His senior thesis topic had been a "solution for the first regional high school in Massachusetts."[7] Interestingly, given Hoover's own wartime work, Hill's initial job had been to design "a fully integrated illuminated ceiling with air conditioning and all that sort of stuff," and during his service in the Korean War he had been "coordinating officer" of "ten million Dollars worth of construction" at Lincoln Laboratory, a federally funded research and defense development facility established in 1951 by MIT. In 1952, Hill was awarded a half-year Gardner Travel Fellowship from MIT before beginning work as a draftsman for the firm of Anderson, Beckwith & Haible and later for Carl Koch and Associates, which invited him to become an associate.[8] The former firm undertook the first of several Lincoln Public School buildings designed in the 1950s. And Carl Koch, despite having designed a few modern houses in Lincoln and having helped form Conantum in 1951, did not concentrate on residential work. Hill's interests became aligned with those of these early employers. In short, his architectural focus supplemented Hoover's.

Hoover and Hill met in Lincoln, where Hill was living by 1953.[9] Although of different generations and trained at different institutions, both shared common architectural ground. Like Hoover, Hill was committed to the modern idiom, which he had learned at MIT. In addition, although Hoover later suggested that his lack of interest and skills in organization and office management led to his forging the partnership in 1966, Hill put the reasons for their association somewhat more expansively: "I think that what probably generated the partnership more than anything else was in just bumping into each other over two or three years, getting into discussions in very informal ways. We found common interests, and we also found divergent interests, and partnerships are god-awful if everybody's the same . . . there's no point in them."[10]

FIGURE 8.2 "Bowling pin sorter" drawing. HBH Papers, Hoover Family.

gant hand, the mechanical function of some of the objects or even the purpose of the drawings themselves remains unclear to a layman. And professionals with technical knowledge, who have examined them, also have questions about them.[10]

For example, one huge drawing, measuring 41 x 30 inches, depicts a basically rectilinear machine consisting of metal armatures and tubing, gears, pulleys, levers, and wheels, yet the directionality of the action, the intended size, and function are undefined (Figure 8.1). It could be a "technical design for presentation for engineers and product design personnel."[11] There is, however, an odd, unexplainable whimsical quality to this drawing with its "roughly triangular shaped box with the weird foot shaped piece sticking out."[12] This element bears a resemblance to another drawing on similar paper in texture and substance, though not color, of what appears to be a bowling pin sorter. (Figure 8.2).

Another drawing depicts a device consisting of a rectangular bar surmounted by an attached cylinder inscribed (faintly on the drawing): "5 [seemingly intentionally unintelligible word] 8 [unintelligible word] 7" across the top with "Use especially with a [unintelligible lines follow]" below. The bar and cylinder are strapped together to a vertical shaft by metal stripping. The whole "resembles an 'rpg,' a rocket propelled grenade, with its tripod in the front to steady it when in use."[13]

A third drawing of an "R2D2-like" object depicts what may be a surveying instrument or perhaps a navigational device such as a gyroscope with levels and dials in its "head" (Figure 8.3). It may have been "drawn from the real object . . . desktop size," showing more than what would be visible from one vantage point, possibly in order to "help one figure out [the] housing of various parts."[14]

Two drawings, like that of the bowling pin sorter mentioned previously, again illustrate identifiable machinery.

In one instance, a paper compactor is carefully delineated and, in the other, a workshop table fully set up with lathe, drill, grinder, and milling machine for metal work, the table's sides buttressed to support a cantilevered shelf.

Five additional drawings seem linked to specific products either promoted to or commissioned by companies: (1) a baseboard radiator, according to an accompanying brochure labeled "International Electrical Heating Division"; (2) a right-angle metal drawer pull identical to one Hoover used in many of his houses (a photograph apparently of the product is attached to the drawing), and pulls stamped LYTRON (q.v.), the manufacturer, have been found; and (3) a cabinetlike console with gauges bearing the company name KELEKET across the top. Keleket X-Ray Corporation produced X-ray apparatus and related supplies as part of Tracerlab of Boston, Massachusetts, founded in 1946.[15]

Drawings (4) and (5) are of a "quick-set hinge" drawn on stationery with the red "pdd" logo; and of a gravel stop edge cleat system or "roof cleat," seemingly from the firm of Product Design and Development, Inc., Waltham, Massachusetts. Promotional material survives for the latter, including an image with specifications and considerable correspondence between Zane B. Laycock, vice president of product design and production, and potential manufacturers.[16] Unfortunately, attempts to locate the firm today or obtain more information about its history have been unsuccessful. The roof cleat seems to have gone into production, for the words "'Lytron' gutter cleat" appear on an elevation plan specifying a particular roof cleat.[17] The Lytron roof cleat and baseboard radiator mentioned above have American Institute of Architects file numbers.[18] Lytron was founded in 1958 by two Lincoln residents, Ernest Neumann and Ferdinand Lustwerk, graduates of the Massachusetts Institute of Technology, who were professor and assistant, respectively, in the engineering laboratory.[19] Although the nature of Hoover's connection with Lytron is uncertain, it seems likely that Neumann, as Hoover's neighbor and close friend, knew of Hoover's work as a designer for Raytheon and of his industrial design interests, and enlisted some of his ideas.[20]

In fact, Hoover and Neumann tried to develop a different, more ambitious product. An eight-page unattributed typed manuscript among Hoover's papers presents "An Inquiry into the Computer Automation of Super Markets." It may have provided the conceptual rationale for Hoover's and Neumann's "BUY YOURSELF," described as a "merchandizing method and the means with which to implement it." That phrase appears on the opening page of the explanatory brochure that further asserted: "It is not considered that Buy Yourself can supplant the retail store. But it can automate economically many aspects of conventional merchandizing as a supplementary facility."[21] The machines

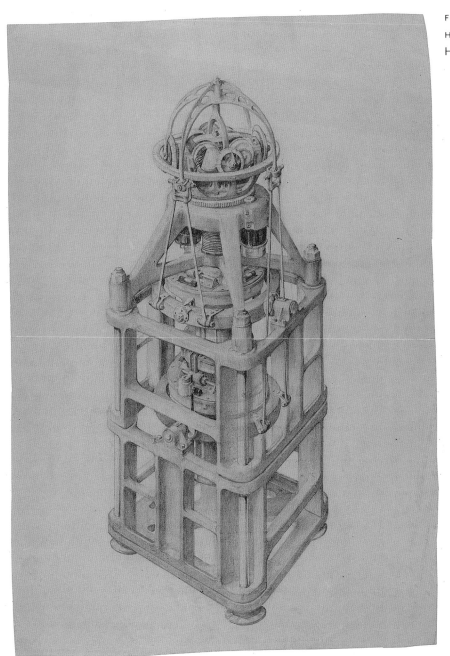

FIGURE 8.3 "R2D2" drawing. HBH Papers, Hoover Family, Hoover Family.

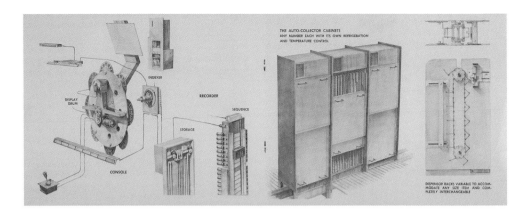

FIGURE 8.4 *Buy Yourself* brochure: "Recorder" and "Auto-Collector Cabinets." HBH Papers, Hoover Family.

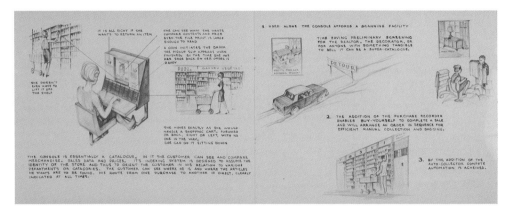

FIGURE 8.5 *Buy Yourself* brochure: Procedure. HBH Papers, Hoover Family.

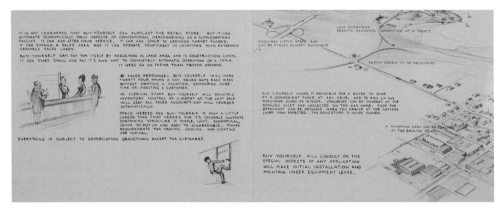

FIGURE 8.6 *Buy Yourself* brochure: Marketing. HBH Papers, Hoover Family.

BUY YOURSELF

FIGURE 8.7 *Buy Yourself*
brochure: Cover. HBH
Papers, Hoover Family.

needed to implement this project consisted of: (1) "Console" with "Indexer" and "Display Drum"; (2) "Recorder" with "Storage" and "Sequence" housed within "The Auto-Collector Cabinets—Any Number Each with Its Own Refrigeration and Temperature Control"; and (3) "Dispensor [*sic*] Racks Variable to Accommodate Any Size and Completely Interchangeable" (Figure 8.4). Hoover's exact, technical drawings of the machinery (those for "Console" and "Recorder") have survived, as well as engaging renderings of consumers and workers (ranging from a "BUY YOURSELF" console operator to an imaginary procession of turbaned male figures bearing gifts or "goods" to tempt a lounging siren) that enliven the brochure's narrative (Figs. 8.5, 8.6, 8.7). Hoover thus made convincing the project that Neumann undoubtedly underwrote and whose business it was to promote. Sadly, Neumann's unexpected death in 1966 put an end to any hopes of the project's development.

Hoover also toyed with commercially producing children's furniture he designed during the Hoover and Hill Associates years. One drawing has survived, that of a simple boxy structure—a chair that might also serve as a table—of wood with a hint of color. Even at the beginning of his residential architectural career, Hoover had designed individual pieces of furniture and furniture-like built-ins that were customized for definite spaces in certain of his houses.[22] However, these later, rare ventures into furniture design are different, for they have no definite "home," but instead add flexibility to an interior. That is, they can live anywhere in any house.

Hoover's curiosity about objects as well as his capacity to conceptualize and make things work, whether as schemes for others to execute or himself to fabricate for his family—a aluminum drawer handle with an obtuse-angled pull, a flat-roofed "modern" doll house for his daughters, skis for his children (could they really have been made of "wood from the basement," as the family recalls?), or very particularized hinged kitchen doors for his son's condominium in Alexandria, Virginia—were constants in his life and career.

FIGURE 9.1 South elevation,
Wade House. HBH Papers,
Hoover Family.

Hoover sustained the quality of his work well into the 1980s. Between 1961 and 1972, he designed thirty-five complete residences spread farther afield than before. Besides three in Lincoln, Massachusetts, houses were built in Leominster, Weston, Lexington, Magnolia, Folly Cove, and Yarmouth, Massachusetts; Thomasville, Georgia; and Miami, Florida; there were nearly twenty renovations; and three residential designs fully realized but never built. Between his last full residential design in 1972 and three years before his death, Hoover carried on a full schedule of renovations that culminated in one final project, a causeway in 1986 connecting an earlier Hoover house and garage. That Hoover was able to maintain a high level of activity for so long is all the more astonishing in light of his massive stroke that ended his partnership in Hoover and Hill. From that time on, he was without a dedicated draftsman, but his work continued as clients sought him out on the basis of familiarity with his work.

That was certainly the case with the Wades, for whom he built a house in Thomasville, Georgia, in 1964. In the 1950s Jeptha Wade III, a lawyer from Cleveland, Ohio, and his wife, Emily Vanderbuilt, both MIT graduates, were living in a turn-of-the-century house in Bedford, Massachusetts.[1] When they decided to renovate it, they remembered seeing Hoover houses on a tour in Lincoln, where they had once rented a house, and commissioned Hoover. Years later when the Wades decided to build a

vacation house in Georgia, they again turned to Hoover.[2] The site, outside Thomasville, was part of a large tract known as Millpond Plantation. Jeptha Wade's grandparents had added ten thousand acres to the plantation in the early 1900s, which in 1960 were divided among the heirs. Wade gave the name "Arcadia" to his share of the estate, which included "one of the largest tracts of virgin longleaf pine in the country."[3] Hoover designed for them a house in a sylvan setting on a knoll overlooking a broad pond.

The WADE HOUSE (1968) is visible only upon a final turn of the one-and-a-quarter-mile drive through a grove of pines (Figure 9.1). The house totaling 2,450 square feet stretches along an east-west axis within sight of a large pond. On the long north and south elevations of the one-story, flat-roofed house, sections of glass and wood are balanced on either side of a central glazed area. The east and west end walls are without fenestration. A shallow plinth of brick emphasizes the sense of the house's rectilinear extension. Hoover specified particular plants at intervals for the low brick terrace formed by the plinth, leaving the surrounding land in its natural state.[4] The house is further "naturalized" through the use of brick for the flooring, fireplace surround, and east and west end walls; and by the use of indigenous long-leafed pine throughout the interior, including the ceiling and ceiling beams.[5]

Two preliminary sketches found among Hoover's pa-

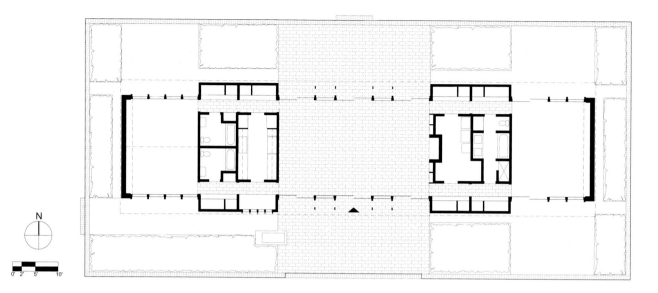

N
0' 2' 5' 10'

FIGURE 9.2 Plan of Wade House.
Drawn by Patrick Rice.
HBH Papers, Hoover Family.

pers illustrate his concern with the definition of the living room.[6] By the final plan, dated June 1964, what he had first conceived as a free-standing fireplace became embedded in a wall in order to create a more substantive barrier between the great room and the master bedroom suite beyond. The resulting design dramatizes the scale of the great room (Figure 9.2). North and south along the main volume are short symmetrical "connective corridors," as Hoover called them. These corridors, like so many of his architectural solutions, function on multiple levels. As they extend beyond the great room, they thicken to provide storage and a small "dining area"; and, at the same time, they open sight lines east/west and ensure unimpeded vistas north/south across the public space. Because of the absence of windows on east and west end walls, natural light in the corridors is low, adding drama to the well-lit great room. In short, the connective corridors enhance the character of the main living volume and accentuate its openness, while protecting the more private areas of the house.

The Wade House is Hoover's farthest removed from Lincoln, one of only two he designed in the far south.[7] In fact, without ever having visited the site and thus experiencing the landscape firsthand, Hoover was able to completely satisfy his clients. Wade wrote, in a letter of 2002:

I have had in mind writing you ever since to let you know how much pleasure your father has given to our family over the many years since he first redesigned our house in Bedford, Massachusetts. That was in the early 60s. In the late 60s, after his stroke, he designed that delightful house in Georgia, which has given us such great

pleasure. Working with him was a wonderfully rewarding experience on both oc-
casions. I'm glad that I've told him so during his lifetime and thought that you too
might appreciate this letter.[8]

Continuing to work through the seventies and into the eighties, Hoover designed his two last complete houses. The RITSHER HOUSE (1972) was commissioned in 1971 by John Ritsher, a public utilities lawyer, and his wife, Cynthia.
The Ritshers decided to look in Lincoln for property, where Ritsher's sister and
his law partner also lived, and where the schools were known to be good. Two
modern houses caught their eye; Hoover had designed both. When four and
a half acres of mostly open fields surrounded by conservation land became
available through Ritsher's law partner, they purchased the land and contacted
Hoover. The house took about a year to build.[9] When it was completed, Cynthia
thought Hoover's interest in solids and voids reminded her of British sculptor
Henry Moore. The house "inspired all our imaginations."[10]

The architect's thought process can be mapped out from a series of drawings that make clear how concerned Hoover was with fitting house to site. One
undated drawing shows a footprint of a rectilinear house penciled in on a topographical map dated February 1970, detailing the land's contours falling away
from a boulder he designated "benchmark/top of ledge outcrop" at one hundred
feet.[11] Another undated drawing shows the same rectilinear scheme with more
clarity. Further drawings dated February 1970 detail north and south elevations
and one floor plan. Then another undated drawing, partially finished on tracing
paper, shows Hoover considering instead a curvilinear scheme. A drawing of
July 1970, labeled "Study for house," develops the same scheme, now in place
around the boulder. Several annotations underscore Hoover's preoccupation
with the vistas from the house.

East view / meadow [directional arrow]; west view / sunset [directional arrow]; kitchen—
view to east / morning sun; View to s.west / Apple trees / direct access to terrace

Further annotations show also his concern with circulation:

Terrace / Direct access to living room, kitchen dining area / Entry—secondary all other /
Sun & shade all seasons / Visual protection from Pike [a neighbor] house / View of apple grove[12]

In the final concept, the "benchmark" boulder became what Hoover called the
house's "pinwheel," around which he spun the vistas (Figure 9.3).[13]

FIGURE 9.3 Aerial view of
Ritsher House. HBH Papers,
Hoover Family.

Interestingly, in 1941 at the very start of his career, Hoover had proposed a design for E. M. Lowe in Port Chester, New York (q.v.) that also used distinct curves. In this project a curvilinear core of two concentric arcs anchors wings that extend at an obtuse angle to either side.[14] Whether the scheme was ever realized is not known, but Hoover kept the plans, each marked "Study," for the first and second floors.[15] Thus the Ritsher House has its antecedents in Hoover's own oeuvre.

The change from an initial rectilinear scheme of the Ritsher House to the pinwheeling one probably owes something to the nearby 1965 residence of architects Mary Otis Stevens and Thomas F. McNulty, which Cynthia Ritsher had admired.[16] She liked the house's fluid space; nothing was squared off, as Cynthia put it, for the elongated one-story floor plan featured several arcing forms. Hoover likely visited the house, for his daughter remembered talking about it with him after

she had seen it. Perhaps his clients' interests and his own taste for experimentation encouraged his use of curved forms. Whatever the case, Hoover's design sprang from a totally different approach from that of the McNultys. Whereas the Stevens-McNulty house seems an abstract construct—curved forms realized in concrete sited on flat, open ground—Hoover's solution was ultimately grounded in unique topographical features of Ritsher's property. Whatever influences were at play, it was surely the boulder as a natural element of the landscape that provided Hoover with the final justification for his design (Figure 9.4).[17]

On arrival, a curved glass wall that wraps around the boulder opens wide to the south view (Figure 9.5). As the entry landing widens, a generous step leads down to the living room. Not until the descent into this space with its great curved fireplace wall is the landscape to the west revealed through a second glazed wall opposite the

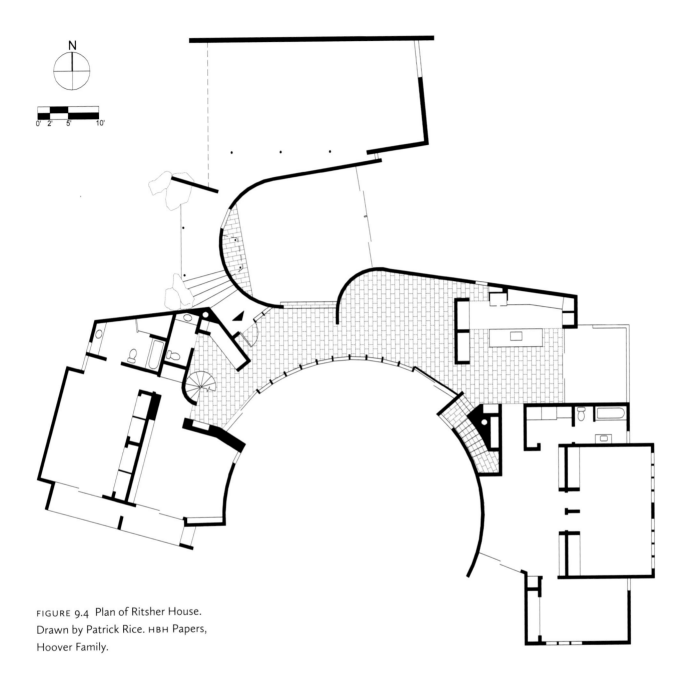

FIGURE 9.4 Plan of Ritsher House.
Drawn by Patrick Rice. HBH Papers,
Hoover Family.

FIGURE 9.5 South elevation, Ritsher House. HBH Papers, Hoover Family.

fireplace.[18] The dining area, in fact part of the arcing circulation path continuing along the curved entrance wall, is nestled behind the convex curve that defines the inner edge of the living room.

Moving from the entry landing past the dining space into the private areas of the house, the arced wall is no longer glazed. The kitchen, playroom and additional bedrooms have windows facing away from the arc to the west. To the east of the great curved entry, a vestibule containing a circular staircase and bath beyond close off that east corner of the house. Windows are reintroduced along the south end of the large study and master bedroom suite.[19] Hoover thus dramatizes light and shade.

Only aerial photography fully reveals the "nautilus shell," as John Ritsher termed Hoover's design. As descriptive as this phrase is, it was not golden-section mathematics but a unique landscape that inspired Hoover's house for the Ritshers.[20] The extent to which he employed arcing forms throughout is exceptional. It is instructive to compare this approximately 4,700-square-foot house with the

Shearer House. In the Ritsher House, through a control of layered curves, complex spatial relations, and control of views, Hoover distinguished contemporary openness from private space, an arrangement realized in the Shearer House by interlocking sectional platforms.[21] The Ritsher House proves Hoover's ability to create distinctive and innovative architecture even after thirty-five years of architectural practice.[22]

In addition to commissions for new houses, Hoover produced many judicious and handsome modifications to existing houses over his career. He approached such projects with respect for the original structure, yet the results always bore Hoover's stamp. Of these, the Heck House of the 1940s remains his most inventive and extensive. However, the house he renovated for his daughter and son-in-law, though far more modest in scale, undertaken almost thirty years later,

FIGURE 9.6 West elevation, Giese House. Period photograph. Courtesy of Lincoln Town Archives, Lincoln, MA.

GIESE   ALTERATION   1974

shows that Hoover considered such projects challenges in problem solving.

Paul Giese, a management consultant, and Lucretia, an art historian, in 1970 acquired a house in Lincoln that had been designed in 1936–37 by Cyrus Winthrop Murphy (1908–71), an architect for H. P. Hood and Sons Milk Company, Charlestown, Massachusetts.[23] The Gieses made the purchase in part because Hoover assured them that the house had potential for the necessary modifications and enlargements they required. The result was the GIESE HOUSE (1974), which completely transformed the earlier Murphy residence.

The property consists of less than one and a half acres near the center of Lincoln, with no principal outlook, although large hemlocks and a diversity of deciduous trees provided pleasant wooded surroundings. The decision to remodel the Murphy House, rather than demolish it, was in part a cost-saving measure and recognition of the house's historic importance. The two-story house totaling almost 2,200 square feet was nearly a cube in plan and elevation with one portion being one story. The structure was flat-roofed and completely planar without ornamentation or overhang other than a small projection over the west-facing entry.[24]

Hoover visually anchored the house to the land by adding broad overhangs that created a strong horizontality. He further enlivened the blocky house by angling exterior walls, reorienting the entry, and creating deep window recesses at ground floor level that generate a play of light and shadow inside and out (Figure 9.6). He clarified and opened up the awkward interior circulation by thrusting out a hall along the entire west

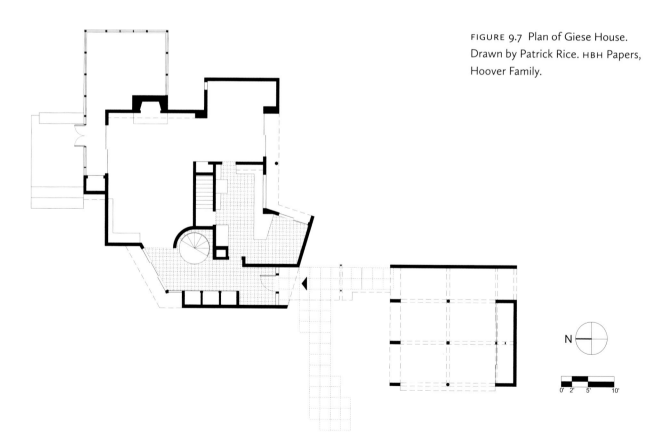

FIGURE 9.7 Plan of Giese House. Drawn by Patrick Rice. HBH Papers, Hoover Family.

FIGURE 9.8 Causeway, Satterfield House. HBH Papers, Hoover Family.

side, which focused entry into the living room and provided room for a spiral staircase within a circular surround. By these interventions, Hoover was able to create greater openness without enlarging the existing living room and adjoining dining area. Hoover further opened up this volume with a sizable, high-ceilinged screened porch to the east, heightening interior and exterior transparency.[25] Upstairs, the original bath and bedrooms were retained and a new master suite added above the now remodeled kitchen; an open balcony from this bedroom enabled direct access to nature. Visqueen roofing on passageway and carport facilitated maximum light in these covered spaces. The Giese House became Hoover-modern (Figure 9.7).[26]

Hoover's unflagging productivity and the loyalty of his clients often drew them back to him. The Satterfields are an example of clients who returned to Hoover, in their case, for a very special project, the SATTERFIELD CAUSEWAY (1986). They invited Hoover to link house (1955) and garage (not designed by Hoover) located a short distance away (see Figure 6.15).[27] Hoover solved this problem by designing an open-sided boardwalk, roofed in Visqueen, that stepped down from the garage on slightly elevated ground to the side entrance of the house. Changing direction three times and accommodating eight different grade levels that follow the contours of the land, the causeway recalls the historic New England propensity to link buildings together against the harsh weather (Figure 9.8).[28]

Nothing even remotely like it exists in Hoover's oeuvre. Its breezy openness and lighthearted yet purposeful articulation of topography enhance the tightly configured house. Perhaps Anne Satterfield's interest in gardening stimulated him to devise a ramp, that most modern of circulation elements, that actually wends its way through the landscape.[29] Charles Satterfield remarked that Hoover "understood people" and was a "psychiatrist," possibly in reference to the delights and demands experienced by a user of the causeway. With this project undertaken just a few years before his death, Hoover decided to express, for what would be the last time, his lifelong commitment to integration of structure and the land.[30]

FIGURE 10.1 Hoover in living
room of 1937 Hoover House.
Period photograph, HBH Papers,
Hoover Family.

10 FINAL WORD

Although he began his career in "collaboration" with landscape architect Fletcher Steele and was intrigued by industrial design, Hoover chose to concentrate on residential architecture. In that realm, Hoover was exceptionally fortunate in the timing of his career, where it developed and flourished, and in whom he found support. Unfortunately for the rest of us, he seldom expressed opinions on architecture in general or on other architects' work and all but never wrote about his own practice or himself. Yet when he did, he was precise, perceptive, and quietly aware of its value.

It is appropriate for Hoover to have the final word:

> Although our house antedated Gropius' we are unknown and our house was out of sight. . . . I am sure my houses do not photograph well inside; the pattern of plan, the quality of light, the visual extension beyond the walls of the house, the break in opaque structures, and the direction of continuity of space inside. If those are sensed at all it can only be by being a part of it.[1]

These sentences sum up the essentials of his practice and Hoover's goals—to create a modern house that in the four seasons of New England is eminently livable and loved (Figure 10.1).

Hoover's determination that house and site should be essentially fused, make sense as a whole, and be responsive to client particulars, caused his houses to be immensely satisfying to those who commissioned them. The daughter of one client, William Shearer, sums up Hoover's achievement with this assertion: "Growing up in this extraordinary house certainly shaped who I became and cemented my visions of humans connecting with the natural environment through built environments."[2] If architecture does indeed have the power to change perception of space and self within created space, Hoover did become, as had been predicted, an architect "worthy of the name."[3] And a modern one at that.

AFTERWORD

Since its construction in 1938 the Gropius House in Lincoln, Massachusetts, has been used as a teaching tool for promoting modern architecture and Bauhaus principles of design, first as the family home of Walter and Ise Gropius, and since 1983 as one of thirty-six house museums owned by Historic New England. Founded in 1910, the organization promotes its mission to preserve and inform about the cultural and architectural heritage of New England from the seventeenth century to the present. Ise Gropius's decision to give the property to Historic New England in 1979 presented an exciting opportunity for the organization to preserve an important example of modernist architecture as well as the architectural legacy of Walter Gropius.

Historic New England was presented a similarly exciting opportunity in 2004, at a time when architect-designed modern houses, sited in the landscape with great sensitivity but modest in size, were rapidly falling victim to demolition. The family of architect Henry Brown Hoover (1902–89) decided to entrust Historic New England with the long-term preservation of the Hoover family home in Lincoln, Massachusetts. The Hoovers' donation of a preservation easement to Historic New England's Stewardship Easement Program was the first to protect a midcentury modern resource, and the Hoovers' efforts brought serious attention to the preservation needs of these unique properties in Lincoln and even nationally.

In 1935, three years before the construction of the Gropius House, Hoover purchased land in Lincoln, Massachusetts, a wooded, rocky upland with a dramatic view over the Cambridge reservoir. At the time, Hoover was working in a landscape architecture firm and wished to establish his own practice as a residential architect. Hoover's home, completed in 1937, was the first of this type to be built in Lincoln, soon to be followed by houses designed by Walter Gropius, Marcel Breuer, Carl Koch, Walter Bogner, and others.

The house launched a successful career for Hoover, who went on to build numerous houses in Lincoln, not to mention those he designed elsewhere, before he retired in the late 1980s. Hoover's aesthetic vision is preserved through Historic New England's preservation easement, which was tailored to his house. This donation has already served as a national model for how, thoroughly and responsibly, to protect other modern homes across the country for future generations to live in and appreciate.

Joseph Cornish
SUPERVISING PRESERVATION SERVICES MANAGER,
HISTORIC NEW ENGLAND

1920–24	B.A., Cum Laude, Department of Architecture, University of Washington, Seattle, WA
	Second Sophomore Honors (1922)
	First Place, New York Beaux Arts Institute of Design (1922, 1923)
	The Auburn Clay Works Prize in Architecture (1924)
1924–26	M.Arch. School of Architecture, Harvard University, Cambridge, MA (on scholarship 1924–25)
	Eliot Prize (1925)
	Eugene Dodd Medal for excellence in freehand drawing and watercolor (1926)
1925–26	Designer/draftsman with Fletcher Steele, Landscape Architect, Boston, MA (part-time)
1926–28	Travel fellowships awarded by Harvard University
	Sheldon Fellowship (September 1926–27)
	Robinson Fellowship (September 1927–May 1928)
1929–37	Designer/draftsman, Fletcher Steele (full-time)
1933–45	Instructor, Lowthorpe School of Landscape Architecture for Women, Groton, MA (part-time)
1937–42	Private architectural practice while continuing with Fletcher Steele (part-time)
1942–ca. 1945	Industrial design work, Raytheon, Waltham, MA
ca. 1946	Private architectural practice resumed
1955–62	Partnership with architect Walter Hill with offices in Cambridge, MA; and industrial design work for Product Design & Development, Inc., Waltham, MA; Lytron, Inc., Cambridge, MA
ca. 1962	Partnership ended due to stroke
1963	Architectural practice resumed. Design Award Citation from the Institute of Electrical and Electronic Engineers (1200 Portable radiometer), design credit Hoover & Hill Associates, Robert Keller
1988	Private architectural practice ended

The Lincoln Public Library addition (1958) was one of the few public buildings Hoover designed. Standing in the center of town, the original structure was designed by renowned Boston architect William G. Preston in 1884. However, by 1958 the Lincoln Library Building Committee recognized a growing population and a circulation rate that greatly exceeded what the Preston library had been intended to serve and voted to build an addition to the original. Believing "good architectural design of the present" could harmonize with that of an earlier period, the Library Building Committee interviewed four architects, three of whom "advocated a contemporary addition."[1] Hoover's design was selected, with the enlarged library reopening on February 2, 1959. While undertaken during the Hoover and Hill years, the addition clearly shows Hoover's fingerprint.

The new building joined the old on Library Lane, a small side road between Bedford and Trapelo roads (Figure B.1). Hoover respected the original Queen Anne revival building by refusing to imitate it. Instead of parroting Preston's gables, curves, and turrets, the planar addition partnered distinctively and harmoniously with the older building. Facing brick over concrete block on the north and east exterior walls resonated with the original brick. The flat roof, extended several feet below the original building's cornice, rectilinear massing, and sheer expanse of window walls, identifies the addition's newness. Hoover reoriented Preston's library by closing the Bedford Road entrance and adding one accessible from Library Lane to serve "patrons who were no longer walking but arriving in automobiles."[2] To the south, a door led into the lobby from an exterior bluestone terrace the full length of the addition. On occasion, the terrace served as a "podium for open-air Memorial Day speakers," reinforcing the library's centrality to the town.[3]

The addition allowed certain library functions to be relocated from one building to the other (Figure B.2). Stacks remained in the old building; a new librarian's office and circulation desk, increased storage, and children's room were in the addition.[4] From the bluestone vestibule and lobby, a half-flight of steps connected the upper and lower floors. Other interior materials were white oak, red birch, and eastern white pine.

About 1967 Lincoln architect Robert Brannen proposed certain modifications for which a freehand drawing exists, labeled "FUTURE ADDITION-UPPER LEVEL."[5] This scheme would have expanded the "childrens reading rm" (so labeled on plan) in a southeast direction, absorbing the entire terrace and outer staircase, nearly doubling the space. It also would have enlarged the original "workroom" to house the town's historical and special collections. However, appropriating the entire terrace for administrative purpose would have compromised the original building's explicit inside-outside relationship on the Trapelo Road side. Brannen's scheme was never implemented.

FIGURE B.1 (*right*) South elevation, Lincoln Public Library. Period photograph. Courtesy of Lincoln Town Archives, Lincoln, MA.

FIGURE B.2 (*below*) Plan of Lincoln Public Library addition. Drawn by Patrick Rice. HBH Papers, Hoover Family.

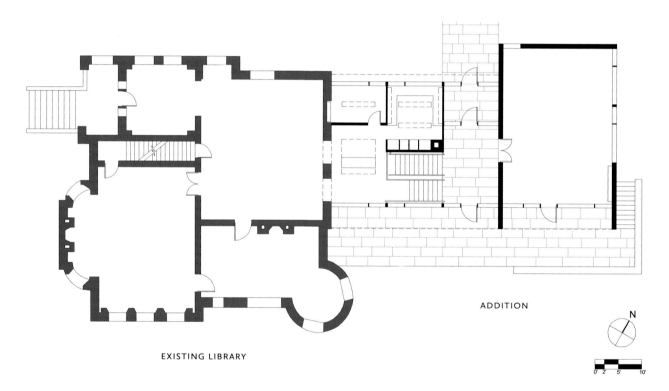

EXISTING LIBRARY

ADDITION

Over time, increased usage forced subsequent changes. Moving the children's room to the lower floor in 1970 freed up space for stacks, while moving the circulation desk to the lobby area on the entrance level provided greater patron access. A climate-controlled vault for storing historical documents with attached study room was added during the nation's bicentennial.[6] In 1988, driven in part by state requirements for handicap access, the Library Building Committee decided to replace the addition with a completely new one designed by architect Graham Gund. While certain modifications might have proved possible, changes of the magnitude the town was seeking by the late 1980s would have effectively destroyed Hoover's design. His addition was demolished in 1988.

Hoover's building was later described in these words: "The contemporary style . . . was simple and sympathetic to the original structure."[7] The tear-down greatly disappointed Hoover, still alive in 1988 and undoubtedly proud of this public building situated in the heart of Lincoln. Sadly, many other 1950s projects by Hoover are no longer extant, for a variety of reasons.[8]

APPENDIX C ARCHITECTURAL PROJECTS

* further information unknown to authors
** Hoover's annotations from his incomplete list of projects

1930S

Henry B. and Lucretia Hoover residence, 1936–37
154 Trapelo Road, Lincoln, MA
altered by Hoover, 1955
  David N. Fixler, "The Modern House in New England,"
  ArchitectureBoston 14, no. 1 (Spring 2001): 37; Matt McDonald,
  "Save Modernist Houses, Friends Beg," *Boston Globe,*
  Thursday, April 8, 2004, 1, 8; Clare Martin, "Early Modern
  Architecture in Lincoln, Massachusetts," *Old House Journal*
  (December 2009) (online); Gary Wolf, "Henry B. Hoover
  (1903 [*sic*]–1989), Henry B. Hoover House," in *Drawing Toward
  Home: Designs for Domestic Architecture from Historic New
  England,* ed. James O'Gorman (Boston: Historic New England,
  2010), 202–3; Abby Goodnough, "Amid Historic Homes,
  New England Moves to Preserve a Modern Heritage," *New
  York Times,* December 3, 2011, A22; Judy Polan, "Staying Home
  & Staying True: A Model for Preserving Modernist Homes,"
  Modernism (Summer 2011): 88; Jaime Gillin, "Preserving New
  England Modern Houses," *Dwell* (February 12, 2012).

Glennon and Elizabeth Gilboy residence, 1939
152 Trapelo Road, Lincoln, MA
altered by Hoover, 1978–79, 1985, 1986–87
  "Wallpaper 'Warms Up' a Lincoln Modern House," *Boston
  Globe* (1950s); David N. Fixler, "The Modern House in New
  England," *ArchitectureBoston* 14, no. 1 (Spring 2001): 38.

1940S

James Walsh residence, 1940 *
Saxonville, MA
  "little house on old foundations/not characteristic/
  OK for clients" **

E. M. Lowe residence, 1941 *
Port Chester, NY
unbuilt

Lockard residence, 1942 *
Scituate, MA
"remodeled vacation cottage" **

Robert and Alice DeNormandie residence, 1947
3 Lexington Road, Lincoln, MA
altered by Hoover, 1981; altered

Gerald and Edith Henderson residence, 1947–48
62 Beaver Pond Road, Lincoln, MA
altered by Hoover

Charles and Gertrude Fitts residence, 1948
40 Weston Road, Lincoln, MA
  "Lincoln Houses to Open Doors to Public," ill. in
  unattributed newspaper clipping, probably the local paper
  The Fence Viewer.

Arthur and Janet Comey residence, 1948
37 Beaver Pond Road, Lincoln, MA
altered

Russell and Anastasia Mahan residence, 1949
158 Sandy Pond Road, Lincoln, MA
altered (unauthorized)

Stanley and Mary Heck residence
(full renovation of 1861 house), 1949–50
23 Bedford Road, Lincoln, MA
altered
  John C. MacLean, *A Rich Harvest: The History, Buildings and*

People of Lincoln, Massachusetts (Lincoln Center, MA: Lincoln Historical Society, 1987), 543, ill. p. 558; William Morgan, "Modern Progression," *Design New England* (September/October 2011): 106–13.

1950S

Dewitt and Morley John residence, 1950
207 Old Concord Road, Lincoln, MA
altered by Hoover, ca. 1955, 1968, and 1972; demolished 2013

John and Mary Peterson residence, 1951
241 Old Concord Road, Lincoln, MA
altered

Maurice and Virginia Shank residence, 1951
233 Old Concord Road, Lincoln, MA
altered by Hoover, 1957; altered

Quincy and Isabel Wales residence, 1952
91 Weston Road, Lincoln, MA
altered

Harold and Ruth Weiss residence (alteration only), after 1952
28 Barberry Road, Lexington, MA

Ernest and Sylvia Neumann residence (alteration only), 1952
146 Trapelo Road, Lincoln, MA

Clarence and Louise Nickerson residence, 1952–53
85 Juniper Road, Belmont, MA

Harold and Eleanor Rheinlander residence, 1952–54
46 Cedar Road, Weston, MA
demolished 2011
    Pamela W. Fox, "The Rheinlander House: Modernism in Weston, 1930–1970, Part II," *Weston Historical Society Bulletin* 41, no. 1 (Spring 2010): 14, 16–17, ill. p. 13.

Andrew and Elizabeth Wales residence, 1953
3 Blueberry Lane, Lincoln, MA

Edgar and Joan Moor residence, 1953
40 Tabor Hill Road, Lincoln, MA
demolished 1996
    Gary Wolf, "Henry B. Hoover (1903 [*sic*]–1989), Henry B.

Hoover House," in *Drawing Toward Home: Designs for Domestic Architecture from Historic New England*, ed. James O'Gorman (Boston: Historic New England, 2010), 204–5.

James and Martha DeNormandie residence (for Mrs. DeNormandie's parents), 1953
14 Old Concord Road, Lincoln, MA

William and Lucy Rand residence (full renovation of existing nineteenth-century barn), 1953
4 Storey Road, Lincoln, MA
altered

William and Yvette Van Huysen residence, 1953
1 Dogwood Lane, Weston, MA
demolished 1994
    Pamela W. Fox, "Modernism in Weston, 1930–1970, Part II," *Weston Historical Society Bulletin* 41, no. 1 (Spring 2010): 14.

Raymond and Suzanne Tunnell residence, 1953–55
48 Conant Road, Lincoln, MA
altered

Albert and Edith Haimes residence, 1954
223 Baldpate Road, Newton, MA
altered by Hoover 1959–60, 1967

William Vanderhout Haut residence, 1954
49 Possum Road, Weston, MA
demolished 2002
    Pamela W. Fox, "Rural to Urban," *Sudbury Town Crier,* January 10, 2002, 13.

James and Ellen Faran residence, 1954
28 Tabor Hill Road, Lincoln, MA
altered

Leopold and Elizabeth Peavy residence, 1954–55
33 Tabor Hill Road, Lincoln, MA
altered

Harold and Ruth Adler residence, 1955
44 Huckleberry Hill Road, Lincoln, MA

Charles and Anne Satterfield residence, 1955; causeway, 1986
38 Tabor Hill Road, Lincoln, MA
altered 1986 by Hoover

William and Constance Shearer residence, 1955
617 Mountain Road, Jaffrey, NH
  Virginia Bohlen, "Their Castle in the Clouds," *Boston Sunday Herald*, July 25, 1965, 30; Alexander Gorlin, "Shearer House, Jaffrey, N.H., 1958, Henry B. Hoover," in *Tomorrow's Houses: New England Modernism* (New York: Rizzoli, 2011), 220–29.

Clarence and Dorothy Abbott residence, 1955
155 High Street, Winchester, MA

H. Philip and H. Stephanie Whitaker residence, 1955
19 Coburn Road, Weston, MA
unbuilt?

Kenneth A. Young residence (alteration only), 1955 *
Lincoln, MA

Alan and Patricia Cole residence, 1955–56
40 Loring Road, Weston, MA
altered
  David N. Fixler and Phyllis L. Halpern, "Life in a Henry Hoover House: The Allen Cole House," in Pamela W. Fox, "Modernism in Weston, 1930–1970, Part II," *Weston Historical Society Bulletin* 41, no. 1 (Spring 2010): 15, 22–24.

Ronald and Charlene Vanelli residence, 1956
89 Woodridge Road, Wayland, MA

Charles and Margaret Child residence, 1956–57
15 Dogwood Road, Weston, MA
demolished 2005
  Pamela W. Fox, "Modernism in Weston, 1930–1970, Part II," *Weston Historical Society Bulletin* 41, no. 1 (Spring 2010): 15.

Richard and Katherine Bolt residence, 1957 (Bolt initially involved)
39 Tabor Hill Road, Lincoln, MA
demolished 2000; rebuilt similar to original design

Robert and Julie Nicholson residence, 1957
60 Baker Bridge Road, Lincoln, MA
altered by Hoover

Alvin and Barbara Schmertzler residence, 1957
23 Peacock Farm Road, Lexington, MA
altered by Hoover, 1964, 1974 for Louis and Barbara (Schmertzler) Osborne

Keith N. Morgan and Naomi Miller, *Buildings of Massachusetts: Metropolitan Boston (Buildings of the United States)* (Charlottesville: University of Virginia Press, 2009), 493.

Karl and Carol Kasparian residence, 1957
36 Huckleberry Hill Road, Lincoln, MA
altered

Lincoln Public Schools, Hartwell School building, 1957
3 Ballfield Road, Lincoln, MA
altered

Daniel and Charlotte Blacklow residence, 1956–59
20 Rolling Lane, Weston, MA
altered
  Pamela W. Fox, "Modernism in Weston, 1930–1970, Part II," *Weston Historical Society Bulletin* 41, no. 1 (Spring 2010): 15.

Loomis and Martha Patrick residence, 1958
33 Crestwood Road, Newton, MA

First Parish in Lincoln, parsonage, 1958
16 Bedford Road, Lincoln, MA
demolished 2014

Langdon and Ruth Wales residence, 1958
18 Moccasin Hill Road, Lincoln, MA
altered by Hoover, 1962

Lincoln Public Library, addition to existing building, 1958
3 Bedford Road, Lincoln, MA
demolished 1988

George and Lucie Flint residence, 1958
84 Lexington Road, Lincoln, MA
demolished 2004

Sargent and Ann Janes residence, 1958
34 Conant Road, Lincoln, MA

Ruth Lyon residence (alteration only), 1958
33 Lincoln Road, Lincoln, MA

John and Joan Carley residence (alteration only), 1958
15 Mackintosh Lane, Lincoln, MA

Arthur and Eleanor Nelson residence, 1958–59
75 Robin Road, Weston, MA
altered by Hoover, 1982–84

Pamela W. Fox, in interview with Arthur Nelson and unpublished Arthur Nelson autobiography, "The Nelson House: Modernism in Weston, 1930–1970, Part II," *Weston Historical Society Bulletin* 41, no. 1 (Spring 2010): 15, 17–19.

Kenneth and Pauline Germeshausen residence, 1958–60
240 Highland Street, Weston, MA
altered
"Island Paradise in Weston: Pool Is Hub of Germeshausen House," *Boston Sunday Herald*, Section 1, June 5, 1960, 16; Pamela W. Fox, "The Germeshausen House: Modernism in Weston, 1930–1970, Part II," *Weston Historical Society Bulletin* 41, no. 1 (Spring 2010): 15, 20–22.

Howard and Ida Wilkoff residence, 1958–61
Land on Woodridge Road, Wayland, MA
unbuilt

Edward and Nancy Rawson residence, 1959
6 Moccasin Hill Drive, Lincoln, MA
altered

Lloyd and Florence Trefethen residence, 1959
23 Barberry Road, Lexington, MA
altered by Hoover, 1973

Edgar and Florence Lee residence, 1959
6 Reservoir Road, Wayland, MA

Homer and Lela Lucas residence, 1959–60
121 Rolling Lane, Weston, MA
altered, demolished 2014
Pamela W. Fox, "Modernism in Weston, 1930–1970, Part II," *Weston Historical Society Bulletin* 41, no. 1 (Spring 2010): 15.

1960S

James and Martha DeNormandie residence (alteration only), 1960s
65 Trapelo Road, Lincoln, MA
room constructed by Hoover from Spencer, MA, Prouty (Martha DeNormandie's maiden name) family house elements

David and Judith Ammen residence (additions only), 1960
61 Baker Bridge Road, Lincoln, MA

Robert and Marion Goldberg residence, 1960–61
119 High Street, Leominster, MA
altered

Stephen and Patricia Crandall residence, 1960–61
(alteration of Crandall's design of 1953)
23 Tabor Hill Road, Lincoln, MA
altered

Thomas and Marianne Witherby residence, 1960–61
20 Huckleberry Hill Road, Lincoln, MA
altered

Eliot and Barbara DuBois residence (alteration only), 1961
207 Sandy Pond Road, Lincoln, MA

Elfriede Maclaurin residence, 1961–62
51 Page Road, Lincoln, MA
altered

Frank and Dorothy Tucker residence, 1961–62
77 Westcliff Road, Weston, MA
altered
Pamela W. Fox, "Modernism in Weston, 1930–1970, Part II," *Weston Historical Society Bulletin* 41, no. 1 (Spring 2010): 15.

Arnold and Fern Abrams residence, 1962
456 Concord Avenue, Lexington, MA

Robert and Shirley Wexler residence, 1962
40 Harwood Terrace, Leominster, MA
altered

Sherman and Ann Kingsbury residence (alteration only), 1963
12 Mackintosh Lane, Lincoln, MA

Lincoln Public Schools, Brooks School building, 1963
3 Ballfield Road, Lincoln, MA
altered

Alvin Schmertzler commercial building (alteration only), 1963
48 Winter Street, Boston, MA
altered by Hoover, 1967–68, 1975, 1980–81

Saville and Anita Davis residence, 1963
Folly Cove, Cape Ann, MA
altered
Nora E. Taylor, "In Xanadu Did Kubla Kahn . . . A Stately Pleasure-dome Decree," *Christian Science Monitor*, December 9,

1964, 25; "Castle in the Clouds," *Gloucester (Mass.) Daily Times*, Friday, September 3, 1965, 7A.

Jeptha and Emily Wade residence, 1964
"Arcadia," Thomasville, GA

Richard and Phyllis Campobello residence, 1964–65
35 Westcliff Road, Weston, MA
demolished 2006
　　Pamela W. Fox, "Modernism in Weston, 1930–1970, Part II," *Weston Historical Society Bulletin* 41, no. 1 (Spring 2010): 15.

Bernard Heyl residence, 1965–66
107 Livingston Road, Wellesley, MA
unbuilt

James Fleck residence, 1966
Todd Pond Road, Lincoln, MA
unbuilt

Bernard and Vera Kopelman residence, 1967
16 Ocean Highlands, Magnolia, MA
altered

Charlotte Donaldson residence (alteration only), 1967
7A Old Lexington Road, Lincoln, MA

Allan and Mary Sandler residence (alteration only), 1967–68
6 Trotting Horse Lane, Lexington, MA
　　Lucretia Hoover Giese and Henry B. Hoover, Jr., with contributions from Anne Andrus Grady, "6 Trotting Horse Drive," *Mid-Century Modernism: Lexington's Second Revolution*, Lexington Historical Society pamphlet, 2008, 24–25.

Kenneth Arrow residence (alteration only), 1968*
"off Mason Street," Lexington, MA
presumably unbuilt

Richard and Phyllis Campobello residence, 1968
Great Island, West Yarmouth, MA
altered

Alvin and Barbara Schmertzler residence, 1968
Sunapee, NH
unbuilt

Everett and Ann Black residence, 1968–70
15 Minebrook Road, Lincoln, MA
altered

James O' Gorman, "Drawing Toward Home," *Historic New England* 10, no. 1 (Fall 2009): ill. p. 15; Gary Wolf, "Henry B. Hoover (1903 [sic]–89), Mr. and Mrs. Everett A. Black House, . . ." in *Drawing Toward Home: Designs for Domestic Architecture from Historic New England*, ed. James O'Gorman (Boston: Historic New England, 2010), 206–7.

1970S

Museum of Fine Arts proposal
for American Wing addition, 1970s
465 Huntington Avenue, Boston, MA
unbuilt

David and Frances Grey residence (alteration only), 1970
33 Barberry Road, Lexington, MA

Mark and Anne Field residence (alteration only), 1970
40 Peacock Farm Road, Lexington, MA

Hershel and Carol Jick residence, 1971 *
12 White Pine Road, Lexington, MS
　　"[D]eck house to my plans/better than deck's hopeless siting would have been" **

Hamilton and Waleska James residence (alteration only), 1971
78 Old Winter Street, Lincoln, MA

John and Cynthia Ritsher residence, 1971–72
16 Conant Road, Lincoln, MA
altered

Raymond and Davina Justi residence, 1972
Miami, FL
demolished after 1972
　　"Privacy When and Where Needed," *Building Ideas* (Fall/Winter 1974/75): 98–100, ill.

Harold Adler housing development, 1972–87
Stratford Way, Lincoln, MA
unbuilt

Bradford and Ellen Cannon residence (alteration only), 1972–73
Scraggy Neck Road, Cataumet, MA
　　Dennis and Anetta Slone residence (alteration only), 1973
　　22 Peacock Farm Road, Lexington, MA

Gerald and Edith Henderson residence (probably alteration only), 1973 *
1801 Main Street, Cotuit, MA

John and Katharine White residence (alteration only), 1973
31 Old Concord Road, Lincoln, MA

Harlan and Ethel Newton residence (alteration only), 1974
37 Lincoln Road, Lincoln, MA

Massachusetts Audubon Society shop (alteration only), 1974
Drumlin Farm, Lincoln, MA

Alvin Schmertzler commercial establishment, 1974–75
Fanueil Hall Market, Boston, MA

Paul and Lucretia Giese residence (alteration only), 1974–76
32 Tower Road, Lincoln, MA
    Andrew Caffrey, "A Reverent Renovation," *Boston Globe Magazine*, June 10, 2007, 64–69.

George and Carol Porter residence, 1975 *
95 Estey Avenue, Hyannis, MA

Kenneth and Emily Bergen residence (alteration only), 1975
20 Mackintosh Lane, Lincoln, MA

Donald and Denise Bienfang residence (alteration only), 1975
2 Tabor Hill Road, Lincoln, MA

Richard and Phyllis Campobello residence (alteration only), 1976
Wianno, MA
further alterations planned by Hoover 1988 but unbuilt

James and Mary Spindler residence (alteration only), 1977
66 Weston Road, Lincoln, MA

John and Jane Felt residence, 1977 *
33 Leonard Road, Sandwich, MA

1980S

Hugh and Sarah Jones residence (alteration only), 1980
80 Ridgeway Road, Weston, MA

Flint residence (alteration to existing house), 1980 *
Lincoln, MA

Martha DeNormandie residence (alteration only), 1981
65 Trapelo Road, Lincoln, MA

Robert and Eliana DeNormandie (alteration only), 1981
45 Trapelo Road, Lincoln, MA

Douglas and Lydia Adams residence (alteration only) 1981
4 Trotting Horse Lane, Lexington, MA

Amy Schmertzler townhouse (alteration only) 1981–83
10 Medford Street, Chelsea, MA

Bruce Adler residence, 1984 (date on existing plan)
Stratford Way, Lincoln, MA
unbuilt

Michael and Kuni Schmertzler residence, 1981–88
Pound Ridge, NY
unbuilt

Robert and Bryce Wolf residence (alteration only), 1982
58 Tower Road, Lincoln, MA

Sylvia Neumann residence, 1982
Land behind 37 Lincoln Road, Lincoln, MA
unbuilt

Bradford and Ellen Cannon residence (alteration only), 1982–83
12 Silver Hill Road, Lincoln, MA

M. E. (Dubin) Speicher residence (alteration only), 1983–84
11 Trotting Horse Lane, Lexington, MA

Gordon and Enid Winchell residence, 1987–88
215 Concord Road, Lincoln, MA
unbuilt

UNDATED OR UNVERIFIED

Bienwind
"nothing" **

James Billings
31 Conant Road, Lincoln, MA
"minor on Conant Road" **

Arthur and Janet Comey
Kittery, ME
"Kittery—Arthur's bad house improved" **

Deane
"simple plan but damaged by sloppy detailing" **

Foell
"not very imaginative site deserved better" **

Maddox
"cleaning up an old house (ca. 1800s) farmhouse" **

Parker Oviatt residence, 1941
"very small house" **

Rodman
"OK for original 3 person family" **

Swain
"nothing" **

Taylor, 1975
"a little remodeling on brick farm house" **

Thiessen
"horse quarters" **

Watertown Savings Bank, Branch #3
exterior plans in Hoover files

NOTES

INTRODUCTION

1. The house in question is one that Hoover designed for Stanley Heck in 1949. It remains today, though modified, in the Lincoln (MA) Center Historic District. See chapter 5.

2. The controversy in effect led to the formation of Friends of Modern Architecture/Lincoln (FoMA/Lincoln), a nonprofit organization in Massachusetts formed to "protect Lincoln's modern houses from destruction and significant alteration . . . provide architectural and historic information and advice to individual homeowners and neighborhoods with modern houses . . . work with various Lincoln organizations, town boards, and citizens . . . [and] to preserve important modern houses and neighborhoods" (Articles of Organization, 2005).

3. For example, Anthony Alofsin, *The Struggle for Modernism: Architecture, Landscape Architecture, and City Planning at Harvard* (New York: W. W. Norton and Company, 2002); William H. Jordy, *"Symbolic Essence" and Other Writings on Modern Architecture and America,* ed. and intro. by Mardges Bacon (New Haven: Yale University Press, 2005); Sandy Isenstadt, *The Modern American House: Spaciousness and Middle-Class Identity* (New York: Cambridge University Press, 2006); Jill Pearlman, *Inventing American Modernism: Joseph Hudnut, Walter Gropius, and the Bauhaus Legacy at Harvard* (Charlottesville: University of Virginia Press, 2007).

4. For example, Thomas S. Hines, *Richard Neutra and the Search for Modern Architecture* (Berkeley: University of California Press, 1994); Adele Cygelman, *Palm Springs Modern: Houses in the California Desert* (New York: Rizzoli, 1999); Justin Henderson, *Roland Terry: Master Northwest Architect* (Seattle: University of Washington Press, 2000); Grant Hildebrand, *A Thriving Modernism: The Houses of Wendell Lovett and Arne Bystrom* (Seattle: University of Washington Press, 2004); James Steele, *R.M. Schindler, 1887–1953: An Exploration of Space* (Los Angeles: Taschen, ca. 2005); Jeffrey K. Ochsner, *Lionel H. Pries, Architect, Artist, Educator: From Arts and Crafts to Modern Architecture* (Seattle:

University of Washington Press, 2007); Thomas S. Hines, *Architecture of the Sun: Los Angeles Modernism 1900–1970* (New York: Rizzoli, 2010); Nina Freedlander Gibans and James D. Gibans, *Cleveland Goes Modern: Design for the Home 1930–1970* (Kent, OH: Kent State University Press, 2014).

5. For example, John Howey, *The Sarasota School of Architecture, 1941–1966* (Cambridge, MA: MIT Press, 1995); Jean-François Leleune and Allan Shulman, *The Making of Miami Beach: 1933–1942: The Architecture of Lawrence Murray Dixon* (New York: Rizzoli, 2001); Andrew Weaving, *Sarasota Modern* (New York: Rizzoli, 2006).

6. Organizations involved with promoting awareness of New England modernism are DOCOMOMO/New England, Historic New England, Friends of Modern Architecture/Lincoln, and Cape Cod Modern House Trust. Publications on modern architects practicing in New England include: Ian McCallum, *Architecture U.S.A.* (New York: Reinhold, 1959), see 170–74 (Carl Koch); Doris Cole, *Eleanor Raymond, Architect* (Philadelphia: Art Alliance Press, ca. 1981); Dianne M. Ludman, *Hugh Stubbins and His Associates: The First Fifty Years* (Cambridge, MA: Harvard University Graduate School of Design, ca. 1986); Gordon Bruce, *Eliot Noyes: A Pioneer of Design and Architecture in the Age of American Modernism* (New York: Phaidon Press, 2007); John Caserta and Lynette Widder, eds., *Ira Rakatansky: As Modern as Tomorrow* (Richmond, CA: William Stout, ca. 2010); and three in which Hoover's work is discussed: James F. O'Gorman, ed., *Drawing toward Home: Designs for Domestic Architecture from Historic New England* (Boston: Historic New England, 2010), 203–7; Alexander Gorlin and Geoffrey Gross, *Tomorrow's Houses: New England Modernism* (New York: Rizzoli, 2011), 220–29; and Peter McMahon and Christine Cipriani, *Cape Cod Modern: Midcentury Architecture and Community on the Outer Cape* (New York: Rizzoli, 2014).

7. Hoover's work is discussed by Robin Karson, *Fletcher Steele, Landscape Architect: An Account of the Gardenmaker's Life, 1885–1971* (New York: Harry N. Abrams, 1989).

8. Aida Wong, Hoover house owner, statement to the authors, June 3, 2011.

9. Hoover endlessly with great amusement retold the tale of once receiving a letter addressed to "H.B. Hoover Trapelord."

1 EDUCATION

1. Letter of Carl F. Gould to George H. Edgell, April 1, 1924. (Harvard University [hereafter HU]. Graduate School of Design. Student Folders (graduate), 1893–1986 (inclusive). UAV 322.282. Folder Hoover, H. B. Harvard University Archives [hereafter HA]).

2. For information on the Beaux-Arts system in the United States, see John F. Harbeson, *The Study of Architectural Design, with Special Reference to the Program of the Beaux-Arts Institute of Design* (New York: Pencil Points Press, 1927, first printed 1926); and Arthur Clason Weatherhead, *The History of Collegiate Education in Architecture in the United States* (Los Angeles, California, 1941), 76–81. See also Norman J. Johnston, *The College of Architecture and Urban Planning, Seventy-five Years at the University of Washington: A Personal View* (Seattle: University of Washington, 1991). We thank Jeffrey Ochsner and Elizabeth Grossman for bringing these titles to our attention.

3. Paul Cret, quoted in Elizabeth G. Grossman, *The Civic Architecture of Paul Cret* (New York: Cambridge University Press, 1996), 200. We are also grateful to Elizabeth Grossman for alerting us to this statement by Cret. Joseph Hudnut, Harvard's Graduate School of Design dean, when appointed in 1936 railed against the Beaux-Arts tradition, which had gripped Harvard previously, calling for its end. For further details, see Anthony Alofsin, *The Struggle for Modernism: Architecture, Landscape Architecture, and City Planning at Harvard* (New York: W. W. Norton and Company, 2002), 154–55.

4. The phrase is from Alofsin, *The Struggle for Modernism*, 8.

5. University of Washington, *Catalogue of Instruction*, College of Fine Arts, Architecture (1924–25), 130.

6. Quoted in Jeffrey Karl Ochsner, *Lionel H. Pries, Architect, Architect, Educator: From Arts and Crafts to Modern Architecture* (Seattle: University of Washington Press, 2007), 135.

7. It is likely that these were made as an undergraduate exercise, though for what specific course is not known. Hoover's son-in-law, Paul E. Giese, recalls Hoover explaining that these drawings were made from memory after the student was shown a photograph. Hoover's University of Washington transcript does not include the one course cited in the catalogue for 1923–24 that involved "sketches of architectural subjects . . .

from photograph," and there are relatively few drawings of the same size as Hoover's "Pantheon" among the student material preserved in the University of Washington Special Collections Archives; student design projects were primarily retained. But it could have been an exercise for a history course, and "History of Architecture" is listed on Hoover's transcript. (We thank Jeffrey Ochsner for information provided in emails to the authors, December 26, 2013, April 9 and July 26, 2014.) Hoover's Harvard transcript indicates that he took several courses labeled "Sketches" for which he received high grades, but it has not been possible to find definite information concerning requirements.

8. Ochsner, *Lionel H. Pries*, 135, 136, fig. 7.1.

9. The architecture department's Suzzallo Library opened in 1926, two years after Hoover had graduated. Deanna Duff, "Architecture at One Hundred," *Columns, the University of Washington Alumni Magazine* (September 2014): 17.

10. Weatherhead, "Important Factors in the École which Influenced Education in the United States," in *The History of Collegiate Education*, 20, 21.

11. The phrase is part of the subtitle of Harbeson's *The Study of Architectural Design*, 1.

12. Ibid., 179.

13. Ibid., 191.

14. Ibid., 299.

15. Paul Cret, "Modern Architecture," in *The Significance of the Fine Arts*, published under the Committee on Education, American Institute of Architects (Boston: Marshall Jones Co., 1923), cited in Harbeson, *The Study of Architectural Design*.

16. Paul Goldberger, *Why Architecture Matters* (New Haven: Yale University Press, 2009), 130, repeats that, for École students, "the ability to create a clear, logical, and elegant plan was considered as important as any aspect of designing a building. The Beaux-Arts architect believed that from a good plan, other good elements logically flowed, . . . It was the document that ordered the spaces in the architect's mind and translated that order and logic into the actual exercise of being in a building." Well thought out spatial arrangement mattered more than the effect of Classical and Renaissance architectural elements.

17. On this subject, see also Ochsner, *Lionel H. Pries*, 18–19, 135.

18. Hoover's student drawings made while at the University of Washington indicate that he was well versed in historical styles. For instance, one drawing is of a "medieval interior," another of a market in Venetian style. Still another of an orientalized interior is inscribed "The Decoration of a Cabaret" Class 'A' II Project." We thank Jeffrey Ochsner as well as Kathryn Leonard, Judith Johnson, and J. P. Brigham for providing access

to these drawings in the Special Collections Division, University of Washington Libraries, Seattle.

19. Hoover received various citations in the *University of Washington Daily* while a student. David A. Rash, historian, kindly provided the following information (email to authors, September 13, 2007).

"Students in Fine Arts Receive High Rating" (January 11, 1922, 1) (mention for "A Door Way to a Reading Room," sophomore problem)

"Architectural Student Received High Mention" (April 6, 1922, 3) (Hoover received first place folio copy mention for the facade of a private residence; sophomore-junior problem)

"University Art Work Is Shown in New York" (December 7, 1922, 1) (Hoover received first mention for "An Entrance to a Post," sophomore problem [Rash believes that "the problem was assigned while Hoover was a sophomore but was not returned for local judgment until he was a junior; the first mention was most likely the local rejudgment result rather than the earlier national judgment result."]

"University Students Win National Honors" (April 4, 1923, 1) (Hoover received a first mention for the design of a community bank; junior problem)

20. Alofsin, *The Struggle for Modernism,* 54.

21. The thesis was found among Hoover's papers. The citation "Notes from Killam / p. 154" on at least one sheet references Professor Charles Wilson Killam, a full professor at Harvard by 1924, who taught and wrote on architectural construction methods and materials. An earlier "thesis design" for perhaps a fraternity clubhouse dates from Hoover's senior year at the University of Washington. What is striking is the complexity of the floor plan with its combination of circular, triangular, and rectilinear spaces, including staircases, encompassing an inner, open courtyard. This drawing of 1924 seems to illustrate future architectural concerns of Hoover: siting, spatial junctures, interior flow patterns. (Special Collections, University of Washington Library, Seattle). Hoover's February 18, 1926, proposal for "A Laboratory Theatre" indicates that an "elevation from the street" as well as additional plans and structural details were also required. The latter material was not preserved along with the proposal in the Harvard University Archives (UAV 322.7.4, Box 40).

22. *Architectural Data—Pyrobar Roof Construction* was published by the United States Gypsum Company in 1922. The first edition of the *Handbook describing Berloy* [pressed steel] *Building Materials* was published in 1921.

23. Alofsin, *The Struggle for Modernism,* 54, 55.

24. Fiske Kimball and George Harold Edgell, *A History of Architecture* (New York: Harper and Brothers, 1918). Edgell held a Ph.D. in Fine Arts from Harvard, and Kimball an M.Arch. from Harvard and a Ph.D. in Fine Arts from the University of Michigan. Their collaborative work may have occurred around 1916–17, when Edgell was on the Harvard faculty and Kimball, whom Edgell would label "the best historian of architecture in the United States," held a Sachs Research Fellowship from Harvard. Paul J. Sachs, for whom the Sachs Fellowship was named, became associate director of the Fogg Art Museum, Harvard University, in 1923. In 1936, Edgell recommended Frank Lloyd Wright for an honorary degree at Harvard's Tercentenary celebration. As that suggestion was not accepted, he proposed Fiske Kimball instead. See Alofsin, *The Struggle for Modernism,* 54, 83.

25. Alofsin, *The Struggle for Modernism,* 54.

26. Kimball and Edgell, "Authors' Preface," *A History of Architecture,* xxiii. It is uncertain which of the two (or possibly both) wrote chapters X and XI on Renaissance and post-Renaissance architecture. Another book by a former dean of architecture at Harvard was also in Hoover's study, Herbert Langford Warren's *The Foundations of Classic Architecture* (New York: Macmillan Press, 1919).

27. Hoover printed his name "H. B. Hoover" twice, his initials H B and the words "plan and section of" twice with "central (?)" added once.

28. Kimball and Edgell, *A History of Architecture,* 501–2, passim.

29. Ibid., 560. Further on, on page 564, Hoover made a doodle notation beside a picture of Frank Lloyd Wright's Church of the Unity in Oak Park, Illinois.

30. Ibid., 565.

31. Ibid.

32. George H. Edgell, *The American Architecture of To-day* (New York: AMS Press, 1928; 1970), 3.

33. Ibid., 119.

34. Ibid., 122. Edgell concluded with an observation that suggests some reservation with modernism and has come back to bite it, even though its modern usage has a different source. According to Edgell, modernism is "a style of undeniable virility, bought at the price, some will maintain, of brutality." Describing Wright's own house at Spring Green, Edgell seemingly grudgingly admitted there was "Force there . . . , grace not at all. Whether it be beautiful or ugly, we leave to the individual observer and to posterity. Interesting it certainly is." The adjective "brutal" has come to be associated with modern architecture of the 1960s.

35. Edgell, *The American Architecture of To-day,* 83. Edgell offers no clarification of this term. He seems to employ "modernism"

and "modernist" as nouns to connote style (his word) or practitioner, and "modernistic" and "modern" as adjectives.

36. *Official Register of Harvard University* 23, no. 14 (April 5, 1926, Faculty of the Architecture, School of Architecture, 1926–27): 25.

37. Edgell, *The American Architecture of To-day*, 82, figs. 71 and 72, and 343, figs. 335–37. Also illustrated was Wright's house Taliesin in Springgreen [*sic*], Wisconsin (121, fig. 108).

38. Edgell, "Fine Arts Ib, General Bibliography and Outline" (September 1934), 65, 61. (Edgell, George Harold, 1887–1954, Fine Arts Ib: general bibliography and outline. HUC 8934.128.3.)

39. Edgell also enumerated, in a letter of January 14, 1926, to Dean Clifford H. Moore, Chairman, Committee on Sheldon Fellowships, Hoover's "high awards in design competitions with M.I.T. and with the Boston Architectural Club. His work was [also] selected to represent the School at the Congress of the American Institute of Architects in New York, last spring." (HU. Records from the Committee on General Scholarships and the Sheldon Fund, 1903–69 (inclusive) UAIII.10.60 [Box 15] HA.)

40. *Official Register of Harvard University* 23, no. 14 (April 5, 1926, Faculty of Architecture, School of Architecture, 1926–27), 32.

41. Observation of Elizabeth Grossman to authors, March 8, 2009.

42. Jean-Jacques Haffner, "Extracts from Professor Haffner's Lectures on Modern Architecture Given in Boston, Chicago, Washington," *Cambridge School Bulletin* 2, no. 2 (April 1, 1930): 10. Edgell was a trustee of the Cambridge School.

43. William G. Perry is described as "a Boston architect who had taught briefly at Harvard" (Alofsin, *The Struggle for Modernism,* 57). See also Perry, "French Comrades in America, II, Jean Jacques Haffner," *Pencil Points* 8, no. 2 (February 1927): 75.

44. Letter of J. J. Haffner to "Dean C. H. Moore," February 6, 1926. (HU, Sheldon Fellowship, 1926–27, UAIII.10.60 [Box 15] HA.)

45. Hoover had won other prizes earlier. Edgell declared, in a letter to Hoover dated April 28, 1925: "I am delighted to be able to enclose the check which represents the second award of this Eliot Prize won by you in the last weekend competition. I was more than gratified when our School ran home with both awards. Mes compliments!" (UAV 322.282 HA 12PT). By way of explanation, "The students in the [architecture] school were fortunate in winning several prizes, and the Faculty was especially pleased when the Prize offered actually by the Boston Society of Architects for a long problem, taken by students in Harvard, in MIT, and in the Boston Architectural Club, was won by Henry B. Hoover, of the Harvard School. . . . The Charles Eliot Prize, open to the same group, was won by George Thomas Daub, while the second award was voted to

Henry B. Hoover." Harvard University, "Report of the President and the Treasurer of Harvard College 1924–1925," School of Architecture, Cambridge, MA, 1925, 138.

46. The phrase "call to arms" is presumably the Cambridge School's and the capitalization of the "L" in the word "Landscape" intentional. "Lectures 1929–1930," *Cambridge School Bulletin* 2, no. 2 (April 1, 1930): 6.

47. Jean-Jacques Haffner, *Compositions de jardins* (Paris: Vincent-Fréal & Cie, 1931).

48. Ibid., 22–23.

49. Harvard's graduate School of Architecture was established in 1900. Robin Karson, *Fletcher Steele, Landscape Architect: An Account of the Gardenmaker's Life, 1885–1971* (New York: Harry N. Abrams, 1989), 9, quotes a 1947 letter in which Steele called his "couple of years to [*sic*] the Harvard School of Landscape Architecture . . . a lot of wasted time." On the other hand, the school's adherence to a Beaux-Arts tradition did have influence. Karson (11) asserts that the "[s]eparation of composition from style formed the basis of Steele's landscape education, and it strongly influenced his approach to design. The prominence of composition over style (also a Beaux-Arts precept) was fundamental to his work. For Steele, space-shaping was an intuitive process."

50. Ibid., 291.

51. Inscribed on Hoover's Harvard University "Report on Standing," dated July 11, 1925. (HU, Hoover, H. B., 1924–26, letters, reports, etc., UAV 322.282, HA12PT.)

52. A note among Hoover's papers from Fletcher Steele to "Hoover" dated May 10, 1925, confirms a working relationship by that time. Steele thanks the undoubtedly busy student for having "stood by the other night to get the Wms. College drawings done." Those drawings were for a World War I veterans' war memorial named the "Hopkins Memorial," described by Karson in *Fletcher Steele, Landscape Architect,* 79–80. For this elegantly austere memorial, Steele "combined two large masonry piers and a delicate wrought-iron arch" that, according to Karson, evidently related to unidentified photographs in Steele's copious image albums (79). A similar configuration was later introduced in the Camden Library Theater garden, Camden, Maine. Hoover was involved on that project as well, being by 1928 associated with Steele full-time.

Hoover owned four of Steele's books, Thomas Bridgeman's 1844 *The Young Gardner's Assistant in three parts: containing catalogues of Garden and Flower Seed, with Practical Directions under each head for the cultivation of culinary vegetables and flowers: also, directions for cultivating Fruit Trees, the Grape Vine, &c., in which is added, a calendar to each part: allowing the work necessary to be done in the various departments each month of the year* (address label of Steele, 88 Broad Street, Boston, on the inside cover); Olave Muriel Potter's *The Colour of Rome, Historical, Personal, & Local* (London: Chatto and Winduw, 1914) ("Fletcher Steele/ 7 Water St. / Boston / May 1923" written in pencil on cover page); Clinton H. Blake's *The Architect's Law Manual* (New York: Pencil Points Press, 1924) ("Fletcher Steele / 7 Water St. / Boston / March 1925" printed in pencil on the cover page); and *Dürer, Des Meisters Gemälde Kupferstiche und Holzschnitte* (Stuttgart: Druck der Deutschen Verlags-Anstalt, n.d.) ("ex-libris / Fletcher Steele 1932" label pasted on inside cover).

53. The project is listed under 1924 in Karson's (*Fletcher Steele, Landscape Architect*, 311) replicated, dated client list of Steele's. A reproduction of a Hoover drawing for the Barbour project is dated 1925 (Hoover files).

54. Letter of J. J. Haffner to C. H. Moore, February 6, 1926. (HU, Hoover, H. B., 1924–26, letters, reports, etc., UA III. 10.60, UAV 322.282, HA12PT.)

55. Letter of Hoover to Edgell, July 1927. (HU Hoover, H.B., 1924–26, letters, reports, etc., UAV 322.282.HA12PT.)

56. Hoover's eleven letters to Edgell, dating from November 5, 1926, while en route to Europe, to that of May 9, 1928, written on the next to the last day he was abroad, are with HU Archives. Hoover's requirements for the Robinson fellowship were two *envois*, according to Edgell, whereas "As a Sheldon fellow you have no responsibilities other than an occasional letter to me telling me how you are doing and where you are." Letter of Edgell to Hoover, July 4, 1926 (among H. B. Hoover's papers).

57. Letter of Hoover to Edgell, December 27, 1926. (HU, Hoover, H.B., 1924–26, letters, reports, etc., UAV 322.282, HA12PT.) Among Hoover's papers is a letter of access granted him as a student of architecture from Gorham P. Stevens, Direttore, American Academy in Rome, February 9, 1927.

58. Letter of Hoover to Edgell, September 1927. (HU, Hoover, H. B., 1924–26, letters, reports, etc., UAV 322,282, HA12PT.)

59. Observation of Elizabeth Grossman to the authors, March 8, 2009.

60. Edgell, *The American Architecture of To-day*, 119. Cram wrote a short response to the question "Will This Modernism Last?" for *House Beautiful* 65, no. 1 (January 1929): 45, 88. His qualifying subtitle was "No. Not in itself but it will leave an Influence for Good." Thomas E. Tallmadge's (44) was "Yes, With Europe and New York behind it, it will go over the top."

61. Letter of Hoover to Edgell, February 22, 1928. (HU, Hoover, H. B., 1924–26, letters, reports, etc., UAV 322.282, HA12PT.)

62. Letter of Hoover to Edgell, December 3, 1927. (HU, Hoover, H. B., 1924–26, letters, reports, etc., UAV 322.282, HA12PT.)

63. Letter of Hoover to Edgell, September 1927. (HU, Hoover, H. B., 1924–26, letter, reports, etc., UAV 322.282, HA12PT.)

64. Hoover wrote from Rome: "Only wish there was some way I could record impressions as well as forms. If, at the Piazza St. Peters, instead of making the inevitable sketch of a fountain and part of the colonnade, if I could only show the colonnade all around me and my back against one of the columns." This is virtually what Hoover did do. Letter of Hoover to Edgell, December 27, 1926 (HU, Hoover, H. B., 1924–26, letters, reports, etc., UAV 322.282, HA12PT.)

65. Henry-Russell Hitchcock, "Six Modern European Houses That Represent Current Tendencies in France and Germany," *House Beautiful* (September 1928): 253–55. Hitchcock there cites houses by Le Corbusier and Karl Schneider. When abroad, Hitchcock saw the Weissenhofsiedlung in Stuttgart (1927), which involved architects Mies van der Rohe, Le Corbusier, and Gropius, among others, calling it "no unworthy successor of the Morienval [medieval town in northern France] or the Capilla Pazzi [fifteenth-century chapel in Florence]." See Hitchcock, "Correspondence: The Decline of Architecture," *The Hound & Horn 3*, no. 3 (March 1928): 245. Hitchcock followed "The Decline of Architecture" with four photographs of the NECCO (New England Confectionery Company) Factory in Cambridge, Massachusetts, captioned "The finest fragments of contemporary buildings" (*Hound & Horn* 1, no. 1 [September 1927]: 28–35).

66. Hoover, in an undated letter to his wife while she was visiting her parents in Georgia, suggested that not all Steele's employees were enthusiastic about working in Steele's office: "Perhaps I'm a little blue tonight. Fletcher told Tommy [Thompson] this morning that he couldn't keep him but three weeks more. It's hard to tell how Tommy felt—he has too much pride to let one know. I guess it's no surprise and I know that he's not been satisfied there lately."

67. Newspaper clipping pasted in an album among Hoover's papers.

68. Karson, *Fletcher Steele, Landscape Architect*, 232, 239; ills. 240 and 242. Hoover evidently remained in contact with Steele, for a letter of March 7, 1951, found among Hoover's papers indicates that he and his wife visited Steele, who had suffered a stroke that month. The correspondent T. M. Connelly wrote on Steele's business stationery: "I know how busy you are, but I do hope you and Mrs. Hoover, maybe, can find time to drop in on him for a few minutes. No flowers—he says he is past that stage now!" Karson notes that Steele completely recovered from his stroke; Hoover was more damaged from his, which occurred almost exactly a decade later (ibid., 270).

69. Untitled form filled out by Hoover and stamped at the top "Mar 17 1932." (HU, Hoover, H. B., 1924–26, letters, reports etc., UAV 322.282, HA12PT.) Hoover concluded his "short account of what you have done since you left School" with "Two months this winter in Spain, Yugo Slavia [sic], and Morrocco [sic]."

70. Gary Wolf insightfully interprets Hoover's use of the word "apostate" as a joke "to emphasize (and acknowledge) that it was not standard practice then (or now) for an architectural graduate to go to work for a landscape architect instead of for an architect! Both at that time (I suspect from his comment) and now, there's a tendency for architects to look down on landscape architects to a certain extent, seeing them as members of a less august and less essential profession" (email to authors, March 11, 2009).

2 FLETCHER STEELE YEARS

1. Karson, *Fletcher Steele, Landscape Architect*, xix.

2. Fletcher Steele, "New Pioneering in Garden Design," *Landscape Architecture* 20 (April 1930): 163, 164, 161.

3. Ibid., 170.

4. Fletcher Steele, "Landscape Design of the Future," *Landscape Architecture* 22 (July 1932): 299.

5. Fletcher Steele, "The Temple Garden: The Garden of Miss Mabel Choate, Stockbridge, Massachusetts," *House Beautiful* 64, no. 1 (July 1933): 21. Steele elaborated that the goal of landscape architecture was the design of "well-shaped air spaces between enclosures of various kinds."

6. Steele to Mary Steele ("Dear Jupe") on Naumkeag stationery, dated September 14, 1950 (The Trustees of Reservations [TTOR], Stockbridge, Massachusetts).

7. The designation "Perugino View" also appears on Hoover's drawing and is presumably in reference to the correspondence between Monument Mountain and the low, undulating hills in some paintings of Pietro Perugino (1446?–1523). We thank Mark Wilson, TTOR, for his help in identifying the direction of the view and the distant mountain's name.

8. Karson, *Fletcher Steele, Landscape Architect*, 120–22. In her Acknowledgments (305–6), Karson states: "Henry Hoover certainly knew Steele better than anyone I met. Our many hours of interviews in his home stand out among the most productive and enjoyable to the entire project. Mr. Hoover's memory is matched only by his kindness. I am deeply grateful to him for his support and the wealth of information he shared so generously." Karson was fortunate; Hoover died on January 2, 1989.

9. Hoover only occasionally mentioned the "office" at home, so it is fortunate that Karson obtained more concrete information about Steele's practice when she interviewed Hoover several times in 1987 and 1988. Like most people in the 1930s and 1940s, Hoover worked five and a half days a week. He was therefore at work the day of the 1938 hurricane that felled several trees near his house, returning to an anxious wife with three small children only late that evening. One time he gently complained to his wife that, although others had a holiday, Steele had not given his office the day off.

10. Fletcher Steele to "Harry" [Henry Hoover], letter of August 19, 1932. Fletcher Steele Papers, Rush Rhees Library, University of Rochester, New York, quoted by Karson, *Fletcher Steele, Landscape Architect*, 146.

11. Karson, *Fletcher Steele, Landscape Architect*, 120.

12. Ibid., 122.

13. Architect Gary Wolf, knowledgeable of Hoover's residential architecture, concurs in his essay on the "Henry B. Hoover House," in *Drawing Toward Home: Designs for Domestic Architecture from Historic New England*, ed. James F. O'Gorman (Boston: Historic New England, 2010), 202. Wolf further observes that Steele could well have "been influenced by having a smart, young, up-to-date architect in his office." Email to the authors, March 11, 2009.

14. These listed here in order of execution were architectural elements in landscape settings.

William T. Barbour, Bloomfield Hills, MI—August 15, 1925

J. S. Ellsworth, Simsbury, CT—June 21, 1928 (two), June 23, 1928

Porter Farrell, Westport, CT—August 1929; April 1, 1930; April 10, 1930

Lawrence Buhl, Grosse Pointe Farms, MI—May 1, 1930 [original drawing]

Robert P. Bass, Peterborough, NH—March 18, 1931; March 1932

Camden Public Library, Camden, ME—April 2, 1931; July 3, 1931; August 1931 (two)

R. P. Snelling, Beverly Farms, MA—April 15, 1931

Standish Backus, Manchester, MA—May 14, 1931

Standish Backus, Grosse Pointe, MI—May 23, 1931; March 28, 1932; June 17, 1932

Mrs. Emily B. Swindells, Rockville, IN—July 1931; August 1931

Mabel Choate, Stockbridge, MA—September 1931; March 1932; April 6, 1932

Frederick L. Dabney, Dover, MA—September 1931

Mrs. Frederick T. Pierson, Pittsford, NY—October 10, 1931

Edwin Allen Stebbins, Rochester, NY—October 10, 1931

Angelica L. Gerry, Lake Delaware, NY—October 1931;
November 1931

Wesson Seyburn, Manchester by the Sea, MA—February
1932; February 26, 1932

Effie Everett Winsor (Mrs. John Wood Forbes) CEM LOT
(inscribed), Forest Hills, Boston, MA—September 14, 1932
[original drawing]

This signed drawing among Hoover's papers inscribed "Mrs.
John Forbes / CEM LOT" bears neither date nor indication of
site. We are fortunate to have surmised its location and are
grateful to Elise M. Ciregna, director of sales and marketing,
Forest Hills Cemetery, Boston, Massachusetts, for showing us
the memorial on Pearl Avenue in that cemetery. Not deviating
in any way from Hoover's drawing, the actual memorial
consists of a vessel (lead) with acanthus leaf (?) design on a stone
(granite) pedestal inscribed on the side facing Pearl Avenue
"John Wood Forbes / October 22 1866 / May 7 1921 / his wife /
Effie Everett Winsor / November 2, 1875 / November 14, 1944."
The back is inscribed "John Winsor Forbes / October 23 1900 /
September 5 1931." Ms. Ciregna also produced the approval date
for the memorial of September 14, 1932.

15. However, Hoover told Karson that he considered the
gardens for George and Mary Doubleday in Ridgefield,
Connecticut (1928–32) to be "one of the office's most intriguing
projects." Karson, *Fletcher Steele, Landscape Architect*, 153.

16. Karson mentions Cascieri in ibid. 114.

17. This drawing is reproduced by Karson, ibid., 116. Karson
discusses a three-foot replica of the garden that was exhibited
in Paris (119); whether Hoover's drawing was also shown is not
known.

18. Family lore and supposition support this position.
The guest book at Naumkeag contains the signatures of
Hoover, then Steele, on September 9, 1928. Steele met Mabel
Choate two years before, in 1926, after lecturing to the Lenox,
Massachusetts, Garden Club, near Stockbridge. Thus began a
personal and working relationship lasting until her death in
1958. Hoover and his wife, Lucretia, were guests at Naumkeag in
August 1938 and again as late as October 1948, according to the
same guestbook. We thank Will Garrison, historic resources
manager western region, The Trustees of Reservations,
Stockbridge, Massachusetts, for alerting us to this resource. Ms.
Choate, on Steele's suggestion, donated Naumkeag to TTOR, of
which he was an advisor and committee member.

19. Karson, *Fletcher Steele, Landscape Architect*, 228. The drawing
is with The Trustees of Reservations, Massachusetts.

20. Ibid., 227.

21. Fletcher Steele, "Naumkeag: Miss Mabel Choate's Place

in Stockbridge, Massachusetts, has been Shaped by Two
Generations of Changing Taste," *House and Garden* 92, no. 1 (July
1947): 70. The Blue Steps also did not figure in the draft of that
article (presumably) entitled "Naumkeag Gardens Develop"
(May 1947) (unpublished manuscript) (Fletcher Steele Papers,
Library of Congress, Washington, DC). Karson, however,
attributes the distinctive railing's design to the influence of
the "clean, modern lines Steele had admired in Sweden and an
Art Deco preference for machine-turned curves (*Fletcher Steele,
Landscape Architect*, 230).

22. We thank Miriam B. Spectre, archivist, and Mark
Wilson, archives and research center manager, The Trustees
of Reservations, Sharon, Massachusetts, and Will Garrison,
historic resources manager Western Region, Stockbridge,
Massachusetts, for their making examination of this material
and the plan mentioned above possible.

23. Karson, *Fletcher Steele, Landscape Architect*, 167.

24. The comments appear in the chapter "Going Up, Going
Down Controls Design," in *Gardens and People*, ed. Fletcher
Steele (Boston: Houghton Mifflin, 1964), 93. On pages 81–82,
Steele listed steps in various parts of the world that he had seen,
claiming, "The wandering landscape architect forgets much, but
he remembers steps as other men remember poetry."

25. Karson, *Fletcher Steele, Landscape Architect*, 29.

26. Statement, interview with Joan Wood, architect/
draftsman in Hoover's Cambridge, Massachusetts, office,
early 1960s, February 23, 2009. Joan Wood went on to say that
Hoover's Beaux-Arts training, in her opinion, was retained but
used for a "different idiom." Presumably, that is, modernism.

27. Steele, "Naumkeag Gardens Develop," 1.

3 FIRST HOUSES

1. The stipend was $3,500. Hudnut's letter to Hoover of May
22, 1936, was sent c/o Fletcher Steele. (HU, Hoover, H. B., 1924–
26, letters, reports, etc., UAV 322, 282, HA12PT.)

2. Application letter of April 9, 1938, from Hudnut to Hoover
attached to letter from Hoover to [Henry Atherton] Frost, n.d.
Frost, associate professor of architecture, was evidently In
charge of collecting submissions. (HU, Hoover, H. B., 1924–26,
letters, reports, etc., UAV 322.282, HA12PT.)

3. Letter from Hoover to Hudnut, April 9, 1938. (HU, Hoover,
H. B., 1924–26, letters, reports, etc., UAV 322,282, HA12PT.)
Hoover concluded with saying, "It would be essential to have
the advice and assistance of Dr. Gropius throughout."

4. Letter from Joseph Hudnut to Hoover, April 29, 1938. (HU,

Hoover, H. B., 1924–26, letters, reports, etc., UAV 322.282 HA 12 PT.)

5. The drawing is illustrated and discussed by Wolf, *Drawing Toward Home*, 202–3. Wolf discusses two additional architectural drawings by Hoover (204–7). Unfortunately, the catalogue gives Hoover's birth date incorrectly as 1903 rather than 1902.

6. Wolf, in *Drawing Toward Home*, 202. In this catalogue, Hoover is placed in the company of other early modern residential architects working in the Boston suburbs by O'Gorman ("Introduction," 17, 18) and specifically cited among the more than four hundred architects whose original drawings are in the collection of Historic New England by Christopher Monkhouse ("Architectural Drawings as Works of Art," 34). Wolf discusses two additional Hoover drawings in this text.

7. Hoover's description of the Alhambra appears in one of his many letters written from Europe to Dean Edgell at Harvard. (Letter from Hoover to Edgell, February 22, 1928, HU, Hoover, H B., 1924–26, letters, reports, etc., UAV 322.282, HAPT.)

8. Hoover's "garden" would encompass the entire two-acre site. As a modern residential landscape design, it is a candidate for inclusion in the National Park Service's Historic American Landscapes Survey (HALS).

Unlike Gropius's landscape for his 1938 house, described as indicating Gropius's "greater proximity to the landscape architects who in the late 1930s were just beginning to find a landscape architectural voice for modernism than to the modernist architects who were his own contemporaries," Hoover's design for his 1937 house developed in his head over decades of living with the site; see Eric Kramer, "The Walter Gropius House Landscape: A Collaboration of Modernism and the Vernacular," *Journal of Architectural Education* 57, no. 3 (2004): 39. Hoover seems never to have planned or drawn the grounds in their entirety. Fortunately, the gardens have been professionally documented by landscape architect Jonathan Keep as an integral part of Historic New England's Stewardship Easement for the Hoover House. Hoover's awareness of inside/outside integration, shaping of outdoor rooms, and sensitivity to topography, far more complex at 154 Trapelo Road than at Gropius's Woods End Road site, are in evidence. Fletcher Steele's knowledge of French modern landscape design undoubtedly provided Hoover with examples of modern landscape design while Hoover was associated with Steele (discussed in Chapter 2).

9. Although Lincoln has been described as a town whose post–World War II "efforts to preserve agricultural lands and other open spaces while also developing different approaches to housing . . . placed it in the vanguard of creative planning," what

determined Hoover to choose Lincoln in the 1930s is uncertain. See John C. MacLean, *A Rich Harvest: The History, Buildings and People of Lincoln, Massachusetts* (Lincoln Center, MA: Lincoln Historical Society, 1987), xxi. Two Lincoln sites, John H. Pierce Park and G. C. Tarbell, however, figure on Steele's client list (Karson, *Fletcher Steele, Landscape Architect*, 313). As these citations date from 1930 and 1931, it is tempting to think that Hoover accompanied Steele on investigatory trips. Although Steele was one of the four landscape architects requested to meet with the committee making the decision for the John H. Pierce Park, Robert Washington Beal was the candidate selected. See "Report of the John H. Pierce Park Committee," *Report of the Officers of the Town of Lincoln for the year 1931* (Boston: Daniels Printing Co., 1932), 127.

10. Price per acre of Hoover's land has risen more than five hundred times since the mid-1930s.

11. Hoover is remembered to have made this statement many times; it was repeated to Mary Ann Hales, "A Hoover Historical District: 50 Houses in Lincoln," *Lincoln Review* 3, no. 3 (July 4, 1979): 11.

12. In some later projects, Hoover indicated trees he wanted saved by making penciled-in circle(s) on the plans.

13. Hoover originally may have contemplated low extensions southward from either end of the living room to an indeterminate point. On the house's original floor plan, Hoover twice noted, "Leave broken joints for future wall." One such wall is shown on the 1935 conceptual drawing. Although it resembles to some extent his designs for Steele, Hoover probably wanted simply to frame the view, further integrating house and land.

14. Hoover made various minor alterations, notably the placement of glass bricks, to the plans when he built the house.

15. In the original plan the two vertical posts extended beyond the lintel, whereas in the completed house they were recessed.

16. Homasote is a cellulose-based fiber wall board promoted in 1925 by the newly formed Homasote Company as a building material. Homasote Company website, accessed January 12, 2011.

17. The modern furniture that could be seen in department store displays and museum exhibitions in the late 1920s and early 1930s, and in articles and advertisements in periodicals, bore the names of European designers and Americans such as Paul Frankl, Donald Deskey, and Russel Wright. American manufacturers—such as the Lloyd Manufacturing Company of Menominee, Michigan; Howell Company of St. Charles, Illinois; and the Conant Ball Furniture Company and Heywood-

Wakefield Company, both of Gardner, Massachusetts, which made an ensemble "Living Dining Room Design for Living House" designed by Gilbert Rohde and featured in the Chicago "Century of Progress International Exposition" of 1933–34— produced their work. See Kristina Wilson, *Livable Modernism: Interior Decorating and Design during the Great Depression* (New Haven: Yale University Press, 2004), 48, ill. 1.23; 30, ill. 1.6; 29, ill. 1.5. But Hoover's limited means likely placed such pieces out of reach. His marble-top table design relates to, yet significantly differs from, one illustrated in *House Beautiful* (March 1937), 79, 3, 91. See also John Stuart Gordon, *A Modern World: American Design from the Yale University Art Gallery, 1920–1950* (New Haven: Yale University Press, 2011).

18. The last piece may date from the 1955 remodeling instead of the 1930s. In his 1955 renovation, Hoover kept the 1937 pieces and added 1950s furniture knock-offs and an Eames plywood-and-metal chair. Hoover wrote to his son (n.d. letter) about Frank Lloyd Wright's furniture: "I have yet to appreciate Wright's furniture. Perhaps if I actually saw some in the proper surroundings my ideas would change but it has always seemed to me to be heavy, formal and formidable, faintly ecclesiastic in character."

19. On plans for the 1937 house, Hoover labeled the principal room of the house "living room," suggesting its all-purposeness. There was need for flexibility and lightness. The room off the kitchen, however, he identified as the "maid's room," a function it never had.

20. See Alexander von Vegesack and Mathias Remmel, eds., *Marcel Breuer: Design and Architecture* (Berlin: Vitra Design Museum, 2003), 104; and Thomas Michie in Dietrich Neumann, ed., *Richard Neutra's Windshield House,* (New Haven: Yale University Press, ca. 2001), 72. Well-heeled clients such as John Nicholas and Anne Brown, for whom Neutra designed "Windshield," could afford imported or custom-made modern furniture.

21. Hoover laid the terrace stone himself.

22. Hoover would continue to use corrugated, translucent Visqueen, a polyethylene plastic material, for roofing throughout his career. Visqueen was a new product in the 1950s. The founding company, Visking Corp., in the 1950s branched out to produce a transparent plastic film, with the trade name Visqueen, which among other applications was "a moisture barrier building material." Website "Viskase Companies, Inc—Company History," accessed November 16, 2011.

23. Letter to his son, ca. 1955.

24. In fact, another "first" modern house existed in Lincoln.

This house, designed by architect Cyrus W. Murphy, is discussed under the Giese House. Both that house, assessed when finished at $2,250, and Hoover's, at $4,500, date from 1936–37.

25. Historic New England's Stewardship Program and the Hoover House are discussed with illustrations in Judy Polan, "Staying Home and Staying True: A Model for Preserving Modernist Homes," *Modernism* (Summer 2011): back page (88).

26. Comments from Hoover's partial list of houses with brief handwritten annotations by Hoover (H. B. Hoover Papers, n.d.).

27. Hoover's son recalls his father using these very words to describe the house's footprint on its sloping land.

28. Hoover would use a "winged" footprint as a major design feature in later houses such as Adler (1955) and Ritsher (1972), both in Lincoln.

29. The original ½-inch Super Harbord siding is mentioned on the plans. Super Harbord was a "new type of Douglas fir plywood made with a waterproofed hot-pressed resin adhesive.... [It was] the most significant development in the entire history of Douglas fir plywood.... Production began in January 1935"; see *Plywood in Retrospect*, no. 14 in a series of monographs on the history of West Coast plywood plants (Tacoma, WA: Plywood Pioneers Association, 1974), 4, 5. The exterior cladding was changed at some unknown date to even-width vertical wood siding. Why the direction was changed is not known, but may have been for practical reasons. Super Harbord may not have weathered properly. Its selection by Hoover shows that he was interested in and aware of new materials. In any case the change greatly altered the appearance of the house.

30. The Hoover and Gilboy houses, Hoover's only complete residences designed prior to World War II, reflect his only known use of multilight casement window. Hoover's postwar casements were single large sheets of glass. The Gilboy House's original steel-frame casement windows have survived and are still in place.

31. A drawing exists showing plan and elevation for the "divan" (sofa) and fireplace wall.

32. The plan specifies "Haskelite or Bruce Block" for the living room floor. Haskelite may refer to a manufacturing company, 1917 to 1958, that made bonded plywood; and "Bruce" is a trademarked hardwood flooring.

33. Constance Shearer, wife of client William Shearer III, in an interview with the authors, September 28, 2001, said that Hoover had designed hardware for the 1957 Shearer House (q.v.) master bedroom and the hanging light fixtures in the dining room.

34. "Decades later, in response to subsequent owners' needs, Hoover made several extensive modifications. The kitchen changes were dramatic. The house, designed for a maid, placed the kitchen in a private wing separated from family, the screen porch and the view. By replacing a narrow translucent door with a six-foot glass slider and removing a swinging door, Hoover totally reoriented the kitchen, opening it to the screen porch, the living/dining room, and the view, thus transforming it into a family space. The maid's room itself was converted into a study and a window added that looks out onto the porch. Hoover later undertook a total rehabilitation of the kitchen, dividing the space into distinct functional areas, cooking and dining/entertaining. The owners wanted a room that would be suitable for casual breakfasts, but elegant for dinner parties. Hoover designed a stainless-steel framed granite-topped table that seats eight people and mirrors the shape of the room. Most intriguing to Hoover was the challenge to develop an overhead light fixture that would serve two functions, each with its own switch, to illumine the day in a different manner than the evening. By day, the glow is from a large fluorescent circle. At night, however, incandescent lights become the sun, surrounded with rays of little theatre lights. Hoover redesigned the master bathroom, replacing the tub with a large tile shower. At the same time he saved key period features, including a unique square-tubed towel bar that he had carried home from the fabricator himself in 1939. Hoover upgraded an auxiliary building, not originally his design, used variously as a horse stable and recreation room, to an ancillary apartment. Given these modifications are from Hoover, this prewar modern house may justifiably be called pristine." Barry Solar, email to the authors, January 14, 2010.

35. To cite some examples: Norman N. Rice, "A Double House by Le Corbusier," *Architectural Record* 68, no. 2 (August 1930): 131–32, 133 ff.; Walter Gropius, "The Small House of Today," *Architectural Forum* (March 1931): 266–78; Henry-Russell Hitchcock, "Six Modern European Houses That Represent Current Tendencies in France and Germany," *House Beautiful* 65, no. 3 (September 1928): 253–55, and Hitchcock, "Modern Architecture. I. The Traditionalists and the New Tradition," *Architectural Record* 63, no. 4 (April 1928): 337–49, and "Modern Architecture. II. The New Pioneers," *Architectural Record* 63, no. 5 (May 1928): 452–60; Frank Lloyd Wright, "In the Cause of Architecture. I, The Logic of the Plan," *Architectural Record* 63, no. 1 (January 1928): 49–57, and II, "What 'Styles' Mean," *Architectural Record* 63, no. 2 (February 1929): 145–51, and III, "The Meaning of Materials—Stone," *Architectural Record* 63, no. 4 (April 1928): 350–56, and in later issues, "Wood" and "The Kiln." Also,

Hitchcock published on "Frank Lloyd Wright" in 1928 (Paris: Editions *Cahiers d'Art*).

36. This occasion caused Wright's first trip to Boston. For scant excerpts and description of interest in and reaction to the lecture organized by Eleanor Raymond, see *The Alumnae Bulletin of the Cambridge School of Architecture and Landscape Architecture* 5, no. 2 (January 1933): 4–6. Wright did visit Boston and Gropius at his house in Lincoln in January 1940.

37. About Giedion and Harvard, see Alofsin, *The Struggle for Modernism*, 156–58.

38. Sigfried Giedion, *Space, Time, and Architecture: The Growth of a New Tradition* (Cambridge, MA: Harvard University Press, 1941; 1967), 502. Giedion's text was first presented as Charles Eliot Norton Lectures at Harvard, 1938–39. Jean Ely repeated this framework in 1967 in *New Canaan Modern: The Beginning 1947–1952*, first published in the New Canaan Historical Society Annual, 1967, reprinted in William D. Earls, *The Harvard Five in New Canaan* (New York: W. W. Norton, 2006), 12. Alofsin reappraises these positions in *The Struggle for Modernism*, 156–57.

Giedion blithely ignored the house Eleanor Raymond had designed for her sister Rachel in Belmont, Massachusetts (1931), and the fact that that year it was published as "probably the first modern house in Massachusetts." Overlooked also were many other houses: Edwin Goodell's for Richard Field in Weston, Massachusetts (1931–34); Paul Wood's for George Wells in Southbridge, Massachusetts (1933); Samuel Glazer's for Frederick Gibbs in Brookline, Massachusetts (1936); and founder of Boston's Institute of Contemporary Art, Nathaniel Saltonstall's house for himself in Medfield, Massachusetts (1937). An unbuilt house by architect Constantin Pertzoff, who would later live in Lincoln, won mention in the General Electric Architectural Competition, "The House for Modern Living," *Architectural Forum*" 62, no. 4 (April 1935): 318.

Dietrich Neumann, in writing of the "mild building boom" of modern houses in New England in the second half of the 1930s, intriguingly speculates that "the relative affordability of building in this phase of the Depression may have allowed for a greater risk tolerance among clients and perhaps facilitated the spread of modern architecture in the United States." See Neumann, *Richard Neutra's Windshield House* (Cambridge, MA: Harvard Graduate School of Design, and New Haven: Yale University Press, 2001), 43.

39. "Invisible Modernism," January 22–February 20, 2004, Wentworth Institute of Technology, organized by John Stephens Ellis, AIA, and Gary Wolf, AIA. Architects and dates of houses: George Sanderson (1931); Eleanor Raymond (1931); Paul Wood (1932); Edwin Goodell (1934); William Lescaze (1936);

Hugh Stubbins (1936); Samuel Glazer (1936); Carl Koch (1937); Henry Hoover (1938) [that date was given to the 1939 Gilboy House in the catalogue]; Walter Gropius (1938).

4 WAR YEARS

1. The school's original name—Lowthorpe School of Landscape Architecture, Gardening and Horticulture for Women—was shortened ca. 1924. See Richard A. Schneider, "Lowthorpe," typed manuscript, Rhode Island School of Design Archives, Providence, RI, 1988, 63. The name Lowthorpe was given the school by Mrs. Low in memory of her late husband, Edward Gilchrist Low.

2. Statement by John Parker, Lowthorpe's last president before 1945, when the school was absorbed by the Rhode Island School of Design, quoted in Jane Alison Knight, "An Examination of the History of the Lowthorpe School of Landscape Architecture for Women, Groton, Massachusetts, 1901–1945," unpublished MLA thesis (RISD Archives, Providence, RI), Cornell University, 1986, 44. The school's records no longer exist, apart from some holdings with the Groton Historical Society, Groton, Massachusetts.

3. Karson, *Fletcher Steele, Landscape Architect,* 61.

4. Schneider, "Lowthorpe," 63, 32, 41.

5. Notice for faculty 1932–33 in *Horticulture* 10, no. 22 (November 15, 1934): 414.

6. Reproduced without specifics in Knight, "An Examination of the History of the Lowthorpe School," 78, 157. Also included on the 1937–38 list as critic is Lawrence B. Anderson, another architect living in Lincoln who taught at MIT. The authors thank Kara Fossey of the Groton Historical Society, Groton, Massachusetts, for making Lowthorpe Papers available.

7. *Lowthorpe School / Landscape Architecture / Horticulture,* Catalogue 1942–44, n.p.

8. Schneider, "Lowthorpe," 166 (quoted correspondence of Erna Strasser deVegrar in her "Memories of Lowthorpe," written February 1982).

9. Ibid., 216.

10. Robert Thurston Kent, ed., *Kent's Mechanical Engineer's Handbook,* eleventh ed. (New York: John Wiley and Sons, 1938), autograph signature with inscription, "Henry B. Hoover/ stamped by mistake" over a Raytheon Mfg Co. date stamp of August 15, 1942. Peter Schwamb, Allyne L. Merrill, and Walter H. James, *Elements of Mechanism,* fifth ed. (New York: John Wiley and Sons, 1938), bearing Hoover's signature, "Henry B. Hoover." "Raytheon's Fritz Gross, a talented young engineer, developed the microwave SG radar, a shipboard radar that was far superior to the radar carried in planes because the German submarines could not tune in on their frequencies as they could with aircraft radar." Raytheon Company website: History/ Technology Leadership, copyright 2008–9, accessed October 15, 2009.

11. Otto J. Scott, *The Creative Ordeal: The Story of Raytheon* (New York: Athenaeum, 1974), 110.

12. Ibid., 126. Scott goes on to assert that Raytheon's mass-volume radar production came none too soon. "Raytheon's leap into the production of essential radar . . . on a mass volume basis arrived at a fortuitous moment for the nation" (ibid., 132). "By October 1942 a microwave radar, the SG, had been put into service." See Louis Brown, "The Significant Effects of Radar on the Second World War," in *Tracking the History of Radar,* ed. Oskar Blumtritt, Hartmut Petzold, and William Aspray (Piscataway, NJ: Institute of Electrical and Electronics Engineers, 1994), 126.

13. Ibid., 140. By 1943, in response to heightened Nazi activity in Italy, Raytheon was in full production of radar designed for amphibious forces. To meet increased production needs, Scott says that Raytheon doubled its workspace by sliding new floors halfway in each story of their Waltham plant.

14. Alan E. Earls and Robert E. Edwards, *Raytheon Company: The First Sixty Years* (Images of America Series) (Charleston, NC: Arcadia Publishing, imprint of Tempus Publishing, 2005), 31.

15. "Raytheon's Fritz Gross, a talented young engineer, developed the microwave SG radar, a shipboard radar that was far superior to the radar carried in planes because the German submarines could not tune in on their frequencies as they could with aircraft radar." Raytheon Company website: History/ Technology Leadership, copyright 2008–9, accessed October 15, 2009.

16. Hoover's architectural plans are replete with detail drawings showing structural specifications and design solutions, often at a minute level. Other drawings, without annotation or description, show a remarkable yet clearly defined intricacy. Hoover's post-Raytheon industrial work is examined in a later chapter.

17. Robert E. Edwards, microwave tube development engineer and manager at Raytheon's Microwave and Power Tube Division, agreed that Raytheon's SG designation may have stood for "Seagoing," followed by a sequential letter. Thus SG would be the seventh version of the shipboard radar. According to Edwards, "An early radar was called the SA, for no apparent functional connection, so the letters did not always have meaning" (Edwards, interview with the authors, September 17, 2011, and emails to the authors, February 9 and 12, 2014).

Dorothy Atwood, an architect/draftsman with Hoover and Hill Associates in the late 1950s, recalls that "Mrs. Hoover came into the office and asked if anyone had a copy of the current *Life Magazine* because there was a picture of JFK in the PT boat he commanded on the cover. She said Hoover had designed the boat's antenna" (Atwood, email to the authors, February 17, 2014). Edwards corroborates that Hoover "may well have worked on SO radar antennas at Raytheon," but adds that "Kennedy's PT boat had not yet been fitted with an SO radar when it was sunk."

18. Scott, *The Creative Ordeal*, 180.

19. Robert Edwards, interview with the authors, October 14, 2009, and in an email to the authors, February 9, 2014, told the story of Percy Spencer, an early Raytheon inventor and engineer, having a candy bar melt in his pocket while walking near a magnetron production line. This led him to realize the cooking potential of microwaves and the assignment of engineers to develop a microwave cooking oven, Spencer's patent for the oven being dated November 1945.

5 POSTWAR HOUSES

1. Among the midcentury modern houses in New Canaan, Connecticut, the earliest dates from 1939. Lincoln's stock is even earlier and numerically greater.

2. In a letter to his son commenting on an exhibition of photographs of Hoover houses taken by Phyllis Swift held at the Lincoln Public Library in 1979, Hoover expressed amusement at some people's surprise, even horror, at "the DeNormandies' decision to build 'that kind of house' in Lincoln and at their age." A later house by Hoover, the 1958 George Flint House, also caused some dismay. In the same letter, Hoover observed, "Even such a modest and relatively recent departure as George Flint's little house strained relations in the Flint family." Distaste for modernism has not died; the house was demolished in 2004.

3. On the Flint family land, see MacLean, *A Rich Harvest,* 17, 19.

4. Rhododendrons were later planted for a subsequent owner by landscape architect E. M. Carlhian in 1971.

5. The flooring otherwise was originally cork and asphalt, with concrete in the utility areas.

6. At the request of a new owner, architect A. Osborne Willauer made several later alterations that affected the drama of the living/dining area. Entry was rendered less effective by Willauer, who extended the original foyer closets with an alcove and corner closet, compromising Hoover's delayed, two-step approach. The sense of a spacious bounded volume, so typical of Hoover, was further dissipated by substituting a wider opening between the kitchen and dining area for the original door, which was closer to the entry foyer. Perhaps to compensate for this visual loss in spaciousness, the roofed terrace was incorporated into the dining area in 1970. Also the master bedroom was extended to the south, its wood siding presumably intended to correspond with the original wooden garage doors. Almost a decade later, in 1981, Hoover designed a studio workshop on the west end; and in 2007–8, architect Brooks Mostue made interior renovations, without changing the house's footprint.

7. For information on these and other Hoover projects, refer to Appendix C.

8. Fitts had moved to Lincoln in 1938. From 1942 until his death in 1963, Fitts served in many official capacities in Lincoln, most notably on the Planning Board and as chair of the Board of Selectmen. See later discussion of William Shearer's house for information on the Paine Furniture Company.

9. Numerous examples of fretwork of a generally more elaborate sort figure frequently in Steele's garden work. (See Karson, *Fletcher Steele, Landscape Architect,* passim.) Hoover used fretwork elsewhere in the Fitts House (front hall balustrade, louvered kitchen door, and built-in cabinets below open spaces), as well as in the 1955 renovation of his own house (full-height balustrade above stairs to the basement, sliding partitions between the living room and entry hall, and between the living room and study-master bedroom area), and in the Giese House (end wall of the screened porch) (q.v.).

10. A plan by Hoover shows a "guest suite" with bath on the upper floor and utility room on the lower level. Hoover upgraded the former spaces to an ancillary apartment to meet the developing needs of a live-in parent.

11. This system's first documented use was at Levittown, New York (1947–51), as a means of providing an economic hot water heating system for mass-produced houses built for GIs returning from World War II. Frank Lloyd Wright also pioneered its use in his Usonian houses at the same time. See Dan Holohan, "A Look at Radiant Heating Systems," *Old House Journal* (November/December 2005).

12. Two of the fixtures were in the living area, two in the dining area, and one in the sunroom.

13. Annotations include broad-leafed evergreens, thyme, sedum, Andromeda, and dwarf rhododendron. Hoover's concern with siting remained paramount throughout his architectural career.

14. Caroline Crane, daughter of the Hecks, in letter to Kenneth Bassett of Lincoln, August 17, 2003.

15. Stanley Heck is listed in the 1944 Town Street records residing on Trapelo Road as "teacher" and as "purchasing agent" in 1944–45. His "life-long interest in the arts" led him to the presidency of the Board of Trustees of the DeCordova Museum in Lincoln (obituary notice, *Lincoln Journal*, January 10, 2003).

16. The house was originally built in 1860–61 for John H. Pierce, purchased in 1884 by George Ropes, and passed to Ropes's brother and sister-in-law, Joseph A. and Mary G. Ropes, in 1896. MacLean, *A Rich Harvest*, 535–36, ill. 536 (1860–61 house); 542–43, ill. 558 (1948 house).

17. Town of Lincoln Department of Building Inspector permit, January 26, 1949.

18. Architectural historian Keith N. Morgan described the Heck House in those words for *Buildings of Massachusetts: Metropolitan Boston*, originally slated for 2006. When finally published (Charlottesville: University of Virginia Press, 2009), however, mention of the house was omitted because its demolition was assumed. After Stanley Heck's death in 2003 and the sale of the house, it was nearly torn down. Although situated in the Lincoln Center Historic District, permission had been granted in 2005 by the Lincoln Historic District Commission for its demolition. When the district was established in 1981, the remodeled house was considered a "non-contributing" feature because it was then less than fifty years old. Nonetheless, the decision to demolish it caused much controversy in town. Fortunately, the house was again sold, and the new owners decided instead to make judicious modifications (enlarged service area, added garage space, study and bedroom above) while retaining the public wing of the house and general aspect of Hoover's design. Work under Lincoln architect Brooks Mostue was completed in 2009. This renovation is described and illustrated in William Morgan's article "Modern Progression," *Design New England* (September/October 2011): 106–13.

6 THE PROLIFIC DECADE

1. The built hexagonal projects date from the 1960s: Thomas Witherby (1960, Lincoln, Massachusetts); Robert Wexler (1961–63, Leominster, Massachusetts); and Saville Davis (1964, Folly Cove, Massachusetts). Unrealized projects include Hoover drawings of various vacation-house schemes stamped May 4, 1959; and houses proposed for Howard Wilkoff (1959, Wayland, Massachusetts) and James Fleck (1965, Lincoln, Massachusetts). Interestingly, a Hoover drawing dated 1939, while Hoover was working with Fletcher Steele, shows a hexagon scheme for the

floor of the Orchid Room for Mrs. Randal Morgan (illustrated in Karson, *Fletcher Steele, Landscape Architect*, 233).

2. The Lincoln Public Library project is discussed under Appendix B.

3. For further information concerning the history of Lincoln subdivisions, see MacLean, *A Rich Harvest*, 568. Morningside Lane, a subdivision added in October 1952, was not dedicated to modernism.

4. Woods End Road is composed of houses designed in 1938–41 by Gropius, Breuer, and Bogner on land made available by Lincoln philanthropist and neighbor Helen Storrow. The Gropius House, the property of Historic New England, Boston, has the distinction of being a National Historic Landmark. These three houses as well as one that is not modern make up a local historic district.

5. Adler founded Vectron, Inc., a company that made electro-optical products for B52 planes, and Documat, Inc., which produced high-speed microfilm and photocopy equipment and duplicating machines. In 1960 Adler secured a U.S. patent for a microfilm camera: U.S. Patent No. 2,964,994, Microfilm Camera, "capable of photographing one or both sides of a document," filed June 17, 1957, awarded December 20, 1960 (U.S. Patent Office). (Bruce Adler, interview with the authors, November 20, 2009.) In addition, Adler established Mitrol, Inc., an internationally marketed database management system.

6. All following information about Adler's Lincoln land transaction also derives from the interview of November 20, 2009. Pollard, a Florida resident, summered in Lincoln. See MacLean, *A Rich Harvest*, 544–45.

7. Adler had met Pollard's minimum price of $50,000 with more money than Pollard anticipated.

8. The town approved the subdivision on June 9, 1953 (Lincoln Annual Report, 1953). Adler's daughter, Davina, recalls her mother discovering huckleberries growing on the property and thinking it "a perfect name" for the subdivision (email to the authors, March 13, 2011).

9. Hoover signed the building permit as the architect, March 11, 1955 (Town of Lincoln, Department of Building Inspection).

10. Dr. Karl D. Kasparian, surgeon, was a graduate of Tufts Medical School. Thomas H. Witherby was an electrical engineer at Raytheon in Waltham. Witherby's daughter, Connie, recalled that, when her parents contacted Adler about moving to Huckleberry Hill, the site was so close to the ledge and precipitous, it was considered dangerous to build on (email to authors, November 12, 2009). Adler asked Hoover to look at the land. Hoover assembled a scale model (using toothpicks) to show the Witherbys that a house could be built on the lot.

Noted on the Witherby site plan, March 23, 1960: "Precise location of house to be determined by architect at site. No excavation shall commence without architect's approval."

11. Letter (n.d.) from Hoover to his son.

12. Letter from Hoover to his son, ca. 1954.

13. "Of course, the client is a factor sometimes difficult, unusually unaware, occasionally supportive, sometimes eroding (the addition of plastic mushrooms on the Adler ledge, etc.)." Letter (n.d.) from Hoover to his son.

14. Notations by Hoover on undated, incomplete listings of projects.

15. Letter (n.d.) from Hoover to his son.

16. Earl Midgely, former Lincoln Building Inspector, interview with the authors, November 17, 2009.

17. Letter from Hoover to Harold Adler, October 24, 1979, in which Hoover proposes a comprehensive lot plan for the new development. Plans dated 1984 exist for a house Hoover designed on Stratford Way for Adler's son, Bruce, but it was never built.

18. In another letter ca. 1986 to his son, Hoover wrote: "I am about to withdraw from the Adler land development. Harold wants to do 40 units, condominiums. The Town, Lincoln, wants separate houses, possibly 20. I believe 12 are possible under sanitary regulations, permit [?] statements. I think Harold unwilling to do the kind of job I want to involve myself with. We'll see. I am tired of it unless I can do a worthwhile project."

19. The town approved the subdivision on August 28, 1952 (Lincoln Annual Report, 1952).

20. Charles Satterfield, interview with the authors, June 10, 2008. All subsequent quotations derive from this interview. Satterfield believed Beatrice Emerson was related to Ralph W. Perhaps this is so, because below her name in the Town of Lincoln's tax records for 1953 are listed "Heirs of Ralph W. Emerson" and "Heirs of Edward W. Emerson." Dr. Edward W. Emerson, "Ralph Waldo's grandson," is mentioned as giving advice to new residents of Lincoln just after the turn of the century, in Paul Brooks, *The View from Lincoln Hill: Man and the land in a New England Town* (Boston: Houghton Mifflin, 1976), 223. Beatrice Emerson may also have been the daughter of Hubert J. Williams, from whom Hoover purchased his land. In the "Memoranda of Encumbrances of the Land Described in this Certificate" pertaining to Hoover's land, Hubert J. Williams is cited as mortgage holder and then Beatrice W. Emerson "Conservator et al."

21. Edgar J. Moor's (MIT, class of 1944 and Harvard Business School) wife, Joan, was an MIT research scientist in biochemistry. Claire (Mrs. Robert) Pearmain, interview with the authors, November 5, 2009.

22. Pearmain, also at Harvard Business School, had met Moor through Moor's sister at a family party in Boston. Information from interview cited above.

23. Travelers would often recall seeing this feature of the house high on the hill as they drove westward along Massachusetts State Route 2. The Moor Pavilion is described and illustrated in Gary Wolf, "Terrace for the Edgar Moor House," *Drawing Toward Home*, 204–5 and back cover. Hoover's drawings for that pavilion and his landscape design illustrate his sophisticated attention to siting as well as his exquisite draftsmanship.

24. This number represented the highest percentage of houses for which Hoover was responsible in one area.

25. A letter to Town Planning Board, October 20, 1954, from Crandall, Faran, and Henry Bayard Philips, MIT professor of mathematics, requesting that Tabor Hill Road be made a public way, included the following information: "In residence: Crandall, Faran, Moor, Phillips"; "In construction: Lillie, Peavy"; "Lot owner: Bolt, Brown, Dean, Ingard, Pearmain, Sears." Among the Tabor Hill residents were this impressive lot: Richard Bolt (MIT, professor of physics); Stephen H. Crandall (MIT, professor of mechanical engineering); James J. Faran (Harvard, Underwater Sound Laboratory); Karl Uno Ingard (MIT professor of acoustics and physics); Huson Jackson (Harvard, professor, Graduate School of Design); Leopold Peavy (Harvard, class of 1939, vice president, Tucker Anthony, Inc.); Charles N. Satterfield (MIT, professor of chemical engineering); and Edward S. Taylor (MIT, professor of flight propulsion). Phillips became a de facto resident of the subdivision when he changed the driveway off Old County Road to his house for that already constructed on Tabor Hill.

26. Leo Peavy knew Charles Fitts before moving to Lincoln, and Fitts presumably introduced him to Christopher Hurd, who would have been cognizant of Lincoln real estate opportunities. Elizabeth Peavy, in conversation with the authors, November 2, 2001, and May 29, 2009. All subsequent comments attributed to Elizabeth Peavy come from these interviews.

27. The DeNormandie and Fitts houses are closely related, their plans in some respects being flipped.

28. Elizabeth Peavy also extolled the fact that "every inch of wall is used for storage of some sort," and cited a desk designed by Hoover for the study so that two people could work at the same time.

29. "You'll find many ways to use this excitingly new all-wood material of wood mosaic beauty. It's virtually warp free . . . ideal for use in interior panels . . . sliding doors of cabinets, closets, etc. It comes in 4' x 6', 4' x 8' and 2' x 8' panels, ⅜" and ¾" thick.

It can be nailed, stained, planed, or drilled with ordinary hand tools. See it!" raved an ad in *Popular Mechanics* (February 1953), 267. This material may well be what Hoover used as sliders in the 1955 renovations he made to his own house on 154 Trapelo Road.

30. Both additions are by Boston architectural firm Schopfer Associates LLC with E. Kevin Schopfer as principal.

31. Albert Dietz's subsequent book on the subject, *Dwelling House Construction* (New York: D. Van Nostrand, 1946), remains in print. Its table of contents included construction topics such as "site inspection," "foundation," "framing," and "fireplaces and chimnies [sic]." In 1960 Hoover substantially modified the house the Crandalls—possibly utilizing Dietz's formulas—had designed themselves in 1953 on Tabor Hill Road.

32. Farrington Memorial had been founded by Charles F. Farrington in 1907 as a nonprofit charitable organization located on Cambridge Turnpike, present-day Massachusetts State Route 2. The remaining two out of the Farrington Memorial four acres were acquired by Ingard for his own house (see n. 25).

33. A gabled roof is shown penciled in over a flat roof on plans labeled Satterfield House; these plans are also dated "3/5/56" in red pencil. Additionally, Hoover's plan for a separate never-built garage was judiciously located closer to the house than the garage later designed by architect Peter Thomas. These plans exist in the Town of Lincoln Building Department.

34. The owner went on to call Hoover "a genius when it comes to light. At first I was puzzled by the house's rear orientation to the northwest, but then experienced early morning sun in the master bedroom and kitchen in the dead of winter. The house is always bright, even on the gloomiest of days" (email to the authors, May 25, 2012).

35. Red oak flooring and pickled Philippine mahogany paneling impart a sense of warmth to the room.

36. We thank Elizabeth Grossman for these on-site observations.

37. A separate apartment was completed ca. 1969 by architect Peter Thomas, who was also responsible for the separate garage mentioned in n. 33.

38. Other examples of such sketches include master bedroom suite and study of the Ritsher House (among Hoover's papers), the entire living space of the Schmertzer/Osborne House (among the Hoover papers), and reading room in the Lincoln Public Library addition (in LPL archives).

39. Barbara (Schmertzler) Osborne, interview with the authors, August 12, 2008. All other comments attributed to Barbara Osborne come from this interview.

40. Alvin Schmertzler, in conversation with the authors, September 25, 2011, recalled that Hoover's one-story scheme for a house in Auburndale, Massachusetts, the Schmertzlers were contemplating, could not be built because zoning in the area prohibited such a structure. Ever since the Depression, one-story houses had come to be considered too modest and therefore deleterious to a neighborhood. The Schmertzlers waited for a time, hoping the regulation would be changed. Meanwhile, the extension of the Massachusetts Turnpike (Interstate 90) near the property rendered the lot considerably less desirable to the Schmertzlers, and they built in Lexington instead. Schmertzler further recalled that the Auburndale house's "japonism" was carried over into Hoover's design for Peacock Farm.

The Schmertzlers commissioned several additional projects. These include: a shop in Quincy Market in downtown Boston, and a Chock Full O' Nuts shop on Winter Street, Boston, later part of a complex in 48–50 Winter Street that Hoover remodeled four times more, that involved

> removing a section of the second floor in order to build a staircase to that level, and expose the space to incoming customers and design a stairwell to the basement and developed that space for an expansion to the entire floor. He redesigned the entrance to the building so that the upper floors could be rented, thus making the relatively small building the first one on Winter Street to be entirely rentable. He [also] designed a house—never built—on a property in Newbury, NH, that . . . bridged a stream as well. (Alvin Schmertzler, emails to the authors, September 28 and October 9, 2011)

Hoover also designed a townhouse for the Schmertzlers' daughter (1982, Chelsea, Massachusetts), and a residence for the Schmertzlers' son and daughter-in-law (1981–83, never built, Pound Ridge, NY).

41. In the seventies, Hoover modified three Compton + Pierce houses in Peacock Farm for Allan Sandler, Dennis Slone, and Steven Dubin. Keith N. Morgan discusses Hoover's work in Peacock Farm and cites the Schmertzler/Osborne House in particular in *Buildings of Massachusetts: Metropolitan Boston (Buildings of the United States)* (Charlottesville: University of Virginia Press, 2009), 439.

42. Anne Andrus Grady, "Peacock Farm: An Introduction," in *Mid-Century Modernism: Lexington's Second Revolution* (Lexington, MA: Historical Society, 2008), 20.

43. Ibid., 21.

44. Hoover returned to the motif of a glazed interior atrium in other houses in addition to the Elfriede Maclaurin House

(1960–61, Lincoln, Massachusetts): Richard Campobello House (1963, Weston, Massachusetts); and Dennis Slone House, a Compton + Pierce design Hoover completely modified (1973, Peacock Farm, Lexington, Massachusetts). Hoover also designed houses with open interior courtyards, as in the case of the Homer Lucas House (1958–59, Weston, Massachusetts) and the Everett Black House (1968–70, Lincoln, Massachusetts).

45. For an earlier house in Peacock Farm (Allan Sandler House, 1954, Lexington, Massachusetts), Hoover also employed modules for the "repeated square forms in the living room/dining room (skylights, lighting fixtures, and double lintel posts between rooms); and a repeated staggered 5 ½, 7 ½, 3½ inch sequence for interior and exterior siding." Lucretia Hoover Giese and Henry B. Hoover, Jr., "6 Trotting Horse Drive," in Grady, *Mid-Century Modernism*, 25.

46. The original skylight was flat and the width of the living room fireplace; the replacement (not by Hoover) is larger and barrel-vaulted with vertical ends.

47. One other change Hoover made in 1964 was to extend the master bath farther east creating a Japanese-like space with sunken tub and access through a glass slider to the outdoors.

48. Wood flooring occurs in all other areas of the house. White stucco for fireplace wall and bedrooms completes the restrained palette.

There are at least three other known examples in this decade of wooden ceilings in Hoover houses: Langdon Wales (1958, Lincoln, Massachusetts), Sargent Janes (1959, Lincoln, Massachusetts), and Edgar Lee (1959, Wayland, Massachusetts). Lee remembers Hoover showing him the Schmertzler-Osborne House before Hoover designed the Lees' house. (Edgar Lee, interview with the authors, January 13, 2010.) Later examples are the Jeptha Wade House (1968, Thomasville, Georgia) and the Raymond Justi House (1972, Miami, Florida).

49. Notations by Hoover on undated, incomplete listing of projects. Admittedly, the street façade of the house did change with the addition of the study, but the house's existing interior remained unaltered.

50. She went on to say that she "felt that not only the house enriched my life but knowing him [Hoover] definitely." Barbara Osborne, interview with Molly Bedell, "Henry B. Hoover, Architect," DVD, 2011.

51. Pamela W. Fox, "The Germeshausen House," *Weston Historical Society Bulletin* (Part II) 41, no. 1 (Spring 2010): 20. Polly Germeshausen is reported to have explained, "We were a little bit crazy then."

52. Kenneth Germeshausen kept all receipts and records pertaining to the construction of the house. Fortunately, both he and the present owners have preserved this documentation.

53. This extension continues the upward thrust of the roof beyond the roof's spine but only over the pool area. It is not visible from the driveway level but does appear on Hoover's west elevation drawing. He surely intended that extension to be counted, so to speak, in his design. It effectively shades that area in summer while allowing the lower winter sun to penetrate as far as the house's center hallway.

54. We thank David Fixler for various observations on the house in emails to authors, August 13 and 20, 2014. He adds, "The primary movement through the house is across rather than along the primary axis of symmetry, and that the experience of moving through this sequence of spaces in this fashion allows them to be perceived in a very dynamic and unclassical way. An interesting take on the Beaux-Arts idea of procession with which I'm sure your father had intimate knowledge." Arguably, trajectory through the upper level of the house as originally designed was somewhat constrained by the pool's sliders, though visually it was unimpeded.

55. Statement by the current owners in email to authors, July 16, 2014.

56. Its "rediscovery" by the Hoover family, who did not know its exact location, occurred under fortuitous circumstances. As Hoover's son recalls,

> In 2001 I received a call from someone who said he had recently bought a house in southern New Hampshire designed by architect Henry Hoover. He had noticed my name in a Historic New England brochure and wondered if I were the architect's son. I said I was the son of Henry Hoover. The caller then introduced himself. I knew that voice instantly. He was not only the third owner of the house. He was my college roommate over fifty years ago.

57. Paine Furniture had been founded by Shearer's great-grandfather, Leonard Shearer, in 1835. At Leonard's death in 1864, the company became known as Paine's, John Paine having married into the business. (Obituary notice for William Leonard Shearer III, *Boston Globe*, January 9, 1999, A13.)

58. Constance Shearer, interview with the authors, September 28, 2001. All subsequent quotations derive from this interview.

59. In a realtor's brochure of 1981, the square footage of living space is given as 8,000 with 1,700 for decks and balconies.

60. Shearer's taste is difficult to ascertain. In his foreword to N. I. Bienenstock's *A History of American Furniture* (1970), Shearer commented that the book's "exceptionally comprehensive survey of this country's furniture during the past three centuries" also includes "an out-line of the faltering development of the 'moderne' period." It is unclear what Shearer meant by "faltering," but according to illustrations of his house in its sales brochure of about 1971, there were no

Plexiglas, glass, or vinyl-covered tubular-metal pieces such as those shown in Bienenstock's text, other than a single 1950s plastic pedestal table. However, Paine Furniture Company evidently did sell furniture in the 1950s in the "modern style"; a couch designed by Frank J. Barrett (1912–99) appears in a photograph of a 1957 living room. The full caption reads: "The Modern-style living room in 1957, with a couch designed by Barrett and other furnishings sold by the Paine Furniture Company, Boston." See Frank J. Barrett, Jr., "Portrait of an Architect," *Historic New England* (Fall 2011): 20.

61. By the time the house was finished in 1957, after a two-year construction period, Hoover had washed his hands of the project. Serious structural mistakes made by the contractor responsible for the third floor had been undertaken without Hoover's supervision, leading to load problems. These required the insertion later of a steel I-beam in the kitchen ceiling to support the upper floor, which, contrary to Hoover's design, had not been constructed with a proper understanding of load requirements.

62. For these and subsequent points on the relation of house to Mount Monadnock, we gratefully acknowledge Elizabeth Grossman's on-site observations.

63. The exterior stone flange wall extending from the living room and connecting to the swimming pool's glazed wall was constructed years after Hoover's involvement with the house. It compromised the strong effect of Hoover's living room volume as originally designed.

64. Virginia Bohlen, "Their Castle in the Clouds," *Boston Sunday Herald*, July 25, 1965, 30.

65. The house had two subsequent owners before its current resident acquired the house in 2002. Without essentially disturbing Hoover's intentions, this owner made several upgrades and removed a large ground-floor greenhouse that had been added by the third owner. He restored the pool and terracing, and surrounded the pool with custom-designed tempered glass fencing around the pool terrace.

66. The Shearer House has been placed in good company (for example, Frank Lloyd Wright, Walter Gropius, Marcel Breuer, and Philip Johnson) in Alexander Gorlin, *Tomorrow's Houses: New England Modernism*, photography by Geoffrey Gross (New York: Rizzoli, 2011), 220–29.

67. Carl Koch, interview with Renee Garrelick, Concord, Massachusetts, Oral History Program, August 10, 1992 (Concord Free Public Library). For more on Maclaurin's life and work, see *W. Rupert Maclaurin: Invention and Innovation in the Radio Industry* (New York: Macmillan, 1949).

68. Katherine Maclaurin Staples, interview with the authors, June 26, 2008, and email, February 8, 2014. The houses

designed by Hoover on Old Concord Road (numbers 207, 233, 241) date from the 1950s. One acre of Mrs. Maclaurin's property was placed under conservation easement with the Lincoln Land Trust by her daughter and son-in-law in order to "preserve the wooded rear view that Mr. Hoover had created."

69. Hoover provided a detailed landscape plan, with many plantings specified as to location and type (for example, "Andorra Juniper" and "American Beech").

70. Four preliminary drawings survive among Hoover's papers that reveal a steady evolution of the architect's thought process from initial concept to final design. Only one drawing is dated, inscribed "Hoover & Hill / 4 Nov. 60," and is presumed to be the latest, since it most closely resembles the house that was built.

71. The above-mentioned plan has notations for furniture placement in every room, suggesting that Hoover conceived these rooms not only spatially but also as meant to be lived in. Two free-hand perspective drawings on yellow tissue also show the living room with furniture, but in these, the atrium appears oddly blocked from the living room either by curtains or shoji-like screens half the height of the room. Hoover had drawn similar conceptual interior views, as previously noted in n. 38.

72. Spiro Kostof, *A History of Architecture, Settings and Rituals* (New York: Oxford University Press, 1985), 197.

73. Ibid., 199. Weston, Massachusetts, architect David Sheffield in 1994 made certain changes to the house, which disturbed its "roman" symmetry. The study became a master bedroom suite and bath with adjacent hot tub room added to the west, and kitchen extended by a new screen porch to the east of the house.

74. Colin Rowe, "Neo-'Classicism' and Modern Architecture," in *The Mathematics of the Ideal Villa and Other Essays* (Cambridge, MA: MIT Press, 1982), 121, in discussing 1950s modern architecture's tendency toward a neo-Palladian "cult of the axis," referred to "the domestic interpretation of Mies [van der Rohe] in terms of a latter-day Pompeian amenity." The authors thank Gary Wolf for bringing this reference to their attention.

75. Notations by Hoover on undated, incomplete listing of projects.

7 HOOVER AND HILL ASSOCIATES

1. We thank Dana Robbat for sharing this information from her files pertaining to Hill. Ms. Robbat had been in correspondence with Hill in 2003 (see n. 4, below) and recalls later being told that he died in 2005. The authors' inquiries as late as 2014 to the MIT Alumni Archives, MIT Registrar's Office,

the Archives of the American Institute of Architects, as well as several former partners of Hill, proved unproductive.

2. See Appendix C itemizing Hoover's entire architectural career.

3. Before World War II, Hoover employed a draftsman in his home office at 154 Trapelo Road and again after the war before the Hoover and Hill days.

4. Hoover and Hill "formed a partnership January 1955." Hill, email to Dana Robbat, September 28, 2003. We are grateful to her for sharing this information. The date 1956 is given for the firm's formation in the *American Architects Directory,* 2nd ed., 1962. For information concerning possible earlier associations, see Chapter 8.

5. According to the Registrar's Office, MIT, Hill attended the institution from 1942 to 1943, returning in 1946 to graduate in 1950. According to the *American Architects Directory,* ed. George S. Kyol (New York: R. R. Bowker, 1962), 314, Hill served as a 1st Lieutenant, Army Air Corps, 1942–46, and as a 1st Lieutenant, U.S. Air Force, 1950–52. Hill became a member of the A.I.A. in 1959. The dictionary lists as "Prin. Wks: Lib, Lincoln, & Sch, Scituate, 59; Sch, L & Off & Resrch. Bldg. for Bolt, Beranek & Newman, Cambridge, 60; Sch, Newton, Mass. & Dorms. for Goddard Col, Plainfield, Vermont, 61." The "Millville Notes" from St. Paul's School (vol. . 50, 2, page 77, originally published Summer 1970) indicate that Hill "has been a Research Associate in Education for the Harvard Graduate School of Education, where he is now a lecturer on Education and Urban Planning and Coordination of Field Studies. He has acted as architectural planner for studies of the school systems of many eastern and midwestern cities and has served as Commissioner of Education for the State of Vermont." We thank Charles Sullivan, executive director, Cambridge Historical Commission, for bringing the Millville Notes to our attention. (Email to the authors, May 16, 2012.)

6. In 1950, Gyorgy Kepes, Carl Koch, Ralph Rapson, among others, were also on the faculty, with visiting professor Alvar Alto. See *M. I. T. Bulletin* (June 1950).

7. Information about Hill in Lawrence Anderson interview in William B. Bechhoefer, "The Development of an Architect (Walter Lee Hill)," unpublished document labeled "thesis," Department of Architecture Study Problem (Cambridge, MA: Harvard University, Spring 1966). Hill explained, "The main reason that I now concentrate [1966] on education is that the pertinent political issues, social political issues of this country are being laid at the door of the school, and many of them are being incorrectly laid there." A grainy photograph of Hill of unknown date appears in Bechhoefer's manuscript.

8. Information about Hill's early 1950s positions comes from *American Architects Directory,* 314.

9. Hill is listed as living on Lexington Road in Lincoln in 1953, according to the Town Street Registry.

10. Comments by Hoover and Hill in Hoover interview in Bechhoefer, "The Development of an Architect (Walter Lee Hill)."

11. Email of September 28, 2003, cited in n. 4.

12. Hill, in Mrs. Arthur Nelson interview in Bechhoefer, "The Development of an Architect (Walter Lee Hill)."

13. The use of italics is in the text. Eleanor Nelson, in ibid.

14. Arthur H. Nelson, *Arthur H. Nelson: An Autobiography,* ed. Pamela Nelson (privately printed, 2009), 48, 49–50.

15. Letter from Hoover to his son, n.d.

16. *Architectural Records in Boston* lists the firm as continuing until 1965; perhaps Hill remained at the Eliot Street address until that date. According to John Miller, (q.v.) became Hill and Associates around 1963, Hill and Gillespie in 1964, and Hill and Associates again in 1965 (Miller, email to the authors, July 1, 2011). By 1967, Hill and Associates, Inc., still existed, according to MIT Alumni Register for 1967 (174). In 1969 the firm became Hill Miller Friedlaender Hollander, Inc. The name again changed, to HMFH Architects, Inc., in 1984.

17. Joan Wood, interview with the authors, February 23, 2009.

18. Dorothy Atwood, email to the authors, February 24, 2014.

19. Joan Wood, interview with the authors, February 23, 2009.

20. The following professionals worked at Hoover and Hill Associates, though not at the same time: Dorothy Atwood, Alfred De Polara, Steve Friedlaender, John Miller, Sam Stevens, Joan Wood, and other individuals whose initials are R. W. A., P. A. K., J. E. L., J. F. S., N. N., U. [?] H., and S. A. C. S. This information comes from interviews and from draftsmen's initials on plans of the period. In addition, the name William L. Hall appears on Hoover and Hill Associates letterhead (below a line separating Hoover's and Hill's) on correspondence between R. Langdon Wales and Hill dating from 1958–59 (the authors thank Ruth Wales for access to this correspondence). William Lyon Hall (1929–99) (AIA 1964–68) is remembered as "working under Walter on larger projects," and as a "job captain," leaving the firm by 1964 (Nancy Hadley, manager, archives and records, AIA Archives, email to the authors, January 31, 2012; Dorothy Atwood and Joan Wood, emails to the authors, January 31, 2012). John Miller, while with Hoover and Hill in the 1960s, also recalled Hoover doing some work for Raytheon (John Miller, email to the authors, February 22, 2010). Dorothy Atwood confirms the number of employees as seven to nine (email to the authors, February 3, 2014).

21. Lucretia Jones (1905–86) came to Cambridge, Massachusetts, from Cairo, Georgia, in 1928 at the invitation of her older brother, who having received his Ph.D. from Harvard in 1927 was back there teaching. She attended courses at Radcliffe College (the University Print Series image—Chapter 1, fig. 1.2—has her notes in its margins) and met her future husband, Henry Hoover, or "Herb" as she called him. Lucretia and Herb were married in December 1929 and, audaciously, given the recent stock market crash, decided to honeymoon in Europe before returning to Cambridge.

22. Wood and Atwood interviews, cited above.

23. According to Dorothy Atwood, email to the authors, February 24, 2014.

24. In 1945, the town decided to construct the first of several elementary schools eventually sited at Ball Field Road. The committee of Lincoln citizens and architects involved with that decision included: John Quincy Adams, Lawrence B. Anderson, Walter F. Bogner, Walter Gropius, Cyrus Murphy, Constantin Pertzoff, and Hoover. See *Report of the Officers of the Town of Lincoln for the Year 1945* (Newton, MA: Garden City Print, 1945), 130.

25. Hill entertainingly calls the discussion over the construction of the school buildings "The battle of the flat roofs. . . . [It was] over when we did the first round, at Brooks School [1963–64]. That was the first battleground, we were vindicated by the results." Hill, interview with Robert Filbin, superintendent, Lincoln Public Schools, in Bechhoefer, "The Development of an Architect (Walter Lee Hill)."

The Friends of Modern Architecture/Lincoln-sponsored inventory of modern architecture in Lincoln (2007), filed with the Massachusetts Historical Commission, Boston, incorrectly listed the Lincoln Public Library addition as Hill's. This information was corrected with the MHC in 2008.

26. The precise date of Hoover's stroke is uncertain, but on the basis of many people's memories, including those of some connected with Hoover and Hill, it is assumed that the stroke occurred in the spring of 1963. Its effect was considerable, yet by late 1963 Hoover was back at work, judging from a letter dated November 20, 1963, from Hoover to Dorothy Atwood about work she might do for him. See n. 28.

27. Hill, email cited in n. 4, above, to Dana Robbat, September 28, 2003.

28. Ibid.

29. After offering an hourly wage, Hoover wrote, "Please let me know if this is not satisfactory. As I said before I do not want to interfere with Walter's work in any manner but with [Saville] Davis, [Jeptha] Wade, [Edgar] Moor [work on a garden pavilion dates from 1964] and some continuing work on [Richard] Campobello I will be happy to buy any spare time you have." Hoover to Dorothy Atwood in letter, November 20, 1963. The authors thank Dorothy Atwood for her gift of this letter and plans of several of the projects she worked on.

30. Hill, interview with Hoover in Bechhoefer, "The Development of an Architect (Walter Lee Hill)."

8 INDUSTRIAL DESIGN

1. George Burnell, ICON, Management Consulting/Transition Management, president (ret.), interview with the authors, September 1, 2010, and email, February 3, 2014. All subsequent information on Burnell comes from this interview.

2. Hoover preferred to work without a stable of draftsmen or even a partner, although he did have both on occasion.

3. The date (January 19, 1953) comes from a diary entry by Kendrick's wife and biographical information from Kendrick's resume, both kindly made available to the authors by his son, Philip H. Kendrick. Mrs. Kendrick wrote: "Saturday Henry Hoover called up and asked Jack [John] if he would like to join forces with him on an associate basis. I still can't believe it and I am too happy to live. After 10 years of hoping and praying for just this sort of thing it just happened—quietly and softly. The modest voice on the other end of the line. I hope it is real. I hope nothing happens to make it not so."

4. Burnell had answered an ad Hoover had placed in the *Lexington Minuteman* for a draftsman in March 1953.

5. Burnell remained in contact with Hoover, however, and the two "talked about my joining Hoover and Hill. . . . Twice more we talked about my joining him. Perhaps I should have. We had some interesting chats about Tech-Built and the application of modular construction in the burgeoning school construction arena." George Burnell, email to the authors, February 3, 2014.

6. Joan Wood, interview with the authors, February 23, 2009.

7. Dorothy Atwood, interview with the authors, March 23, 2009, and email to authors, February 3, 2014. See also Chapter 4, n. 17.

8. John Miller, email to the authors, February 22, 2010.

9. Sheets of printed schematic human figures were found among Hoover's papers.

10. The following Information comes from Beth Mosher, associate professor of industrial design, Rhode Island School of Design, after viewing the drawings on March 20, 2009, and a subsequent email of March 25, 2009. We also thank George Burnell, Icon Transition Management, principal (ret.), for his

observations of September 1, 2010. Robert E. Edwards, retired engineer and manager at Raytheon microwave and power tube division, also examined the drawings, on October 14, 2009.

11. George Burnell, in conversation with the authors, September 1, 2010.

12. Beth Mosher, email to the authors, March 25, 2009.

13. Ibid.

14. Ibid.

15. See William O. Faxon, "Tracerlab Incorporated," *Analysts Journal* 12, no. 3 (June 1956): 141. Because Tracerlab had acquired the Kelley-Koett Manufacturing Company of Covington, Kentucky, in 1951, the name of this Tracerlab wholly owned subsidiary became Keleket. "Tracerlab Keleket" is mentioned as among the "cryptic names" of companies that had sprouted along Route 128 by the late 1950s. See Christopher Rand, *Cambridge, U.S.A.: Hub of New World* (New York: Oxford University Press, 1964), 8.

16. Printed advertisements among Hoover's papers indicate that the roof cleat appeared in the March 1964 issues of *Contractor News* and *Heating & Air Conditioning Contractor*. One Zane B. Laycock, NRC, Inc., is thanked by Philip A. Schweitzer, editor, for supplying data on tantalum for Schweitzer's *Corrosion and Corrosion Protection Handbook* (New York: Marcel Dekker, 1989), vi. The person is surely the same.

17. The notation appears on plans for the Edgar Lee House in Wayland, Massachusetts (1959).

18. Filing these "products" with the AIA was not the equivalent of establishing a patent but rather a means of categorizing them. For instance, the file number 12-B-3 located the roof cleat within section 12, "Roofing and Siding other than Wood." 12-B referred to "Built-up Roofing and Siding (including Bituminous, Glass Fiber, Asbestos, Gravel or Slag, Slate or Smooth Surfaced)," and 3 further isolated the product to "Gravel Stop." In the case of the file number for the baseboard heater, 30 refers to "Heating" in general and 30-C-44 to "Radiant Heating (Panel Ceiling, and Baseboard Heating, including Electric and Gas)." In this way the file number printed on whatever brochure existed was "a category number to help group similar products together" comparable to a book's Dewey decimal system number. Nancy Hadley, archivist and records manager, American Institute of Architects, emails to the authors, January 26, 27, and February 16, 2010.

19. This information derives from "A History of Lytron: 50 Years of Manufacturing & Engineering Excellence," accessed from Lytron's website, January 14, 2010. When contacted, the firm was unable to provide further historical details.

20. Hoover did some renovation work on Neumann's house in 1952.

21. This phrase appears in the opening page of the brochure for BUY YOURSELF to explain the product. Several copies are among Hoover's papers.

22. The houses are Hoover (1937), Gilboy (1939), and later Satterfield (1957) and Shearer (1957). The birch wood rectilinear bench in Hoover's own house may be of the same time as his design for children's furniture, the latter apparently also of light wood.

9 LATE WORK

1. Jeptha and Emily Wade, interview with the authors, August 3, 2003. In 2001, the authors received a telephone call from their first cousin in southwest Georgia, stating that she had recently learned that a friend's brother, Jeptha Wade, owned a house designed by Hoover in nearby Thomasville.

2. The Wades reflected on their amicable relationship with Hoover: "Unlike many architects, he looked and listened" (ibid.).

3. Obituary, Jeptha H. Wade, *Thomasville Times-Enterprise*, August 19, 2008. By the name "Arcadia," Wade intended to evoke "rolling hills" (telephone interview, February 14, 2010, with Carroll Weaver, overseer of Arcadia). According to Weaver, the Wades wintered in Arcadia, usually from December through February, the "end of quail season." Wade donated a large part of his land to conservation. "The Wade Tract Preserve: A Window to the Past," *Tall Timbers/Stewards of Wildlife and Wildlands*, website accessed January 23, 2010, explains: "The Wade Tract Preserve is a 200-acre (85 hectares) old-growth research plot managed by Tall Timbers Research Station surrounded by a 3,200-acre (1,260 hectares) private hunting estate near Thomasville, GA."

4. A drawing in Hoover's hand entitled "Soil Preparation and Planting Layout" attests to Hoover's care in presenting this house in a natural setting. On the floor plan, Hoover even wrote: "Locate trees and plant beds."

5. An elevation for the fireplace wall shows the fireplace labeled "Brick" with "13 courses" of brick for its height.

6. Dorothy Atwood kindly gave the final plans to the Hoover family in 2009.

7. The other "southern" house Hoover designed, later demolished, was in 1972 for Raymond Justi of Miami, Florida.

8. Jeptha Wade, in letter to the authors, October 15, 2002. Wade had been informed of the names of Hoover's children by their first cousin in Georgia.

9. The Ritshers budgeted $125,000 for the house, but when Hoover estimated it would be $150,000, agreed. In fact, the house came in at around $140,000. Ritsher further noted that two banks had turned down the financing of the house because the design was "too radical." John Ritsher, interview with the authors, July 29, 2009.

10. Cynthia Ritsher, interview with the authors, May 15, 2009.

11. "RITSHER DISCARDED SCHEME" is noted on the reverse of the topographical map, not in Hoover's hand.

12. Hoover's son recalls his father mentioning that the fenestration of the house was to reveal only nature, though the house was in a lightly residential area.

13. The term "pinwheel" recalls Giedion's assertion that Bauhaus architecture "expands into a pin wheel." This comment is quoted by Rowe in discussion of "peripheric composition," which he contrasts with neo-Palladian centralization. Besides Bauhaus work, Rowe cites in particular Mies's 1929 Barcelona Pavilion in Spain and Le Corbusier's 1928 Villa Stein in Garches, France, as examples of spatial decentralization in modern architectural (Rowe, "Neo-'Classicism' and Modern Architecture," 128). Hoover's "composition," however, is likely to have had more to do with site than theory. The authors thank Gary Wolf for bringing this essay to their attention. John Ritsher told the story of Hoover's decision, during house construction, to move a living room wall in order to frame, not block, a view of a large pear tree. The tree later died.

14. The two existing plans (first and second floors) of the house are labeled in Hoover's hand "Study-House for E. M. Lowe Esq. / Portchester [sic], New York," and "Henry B Hoover Architect / Boston Massachusetts Jan 1941." See Chapter 3 for earlier mention of this house.

15. The Lowe House appears to be Hoover's first full two-story design.

16. The Stevens-McNulty House, demolished in 2001, was described in *Architectural Forum*, November 1965, and subsequently in French and German architectural periodicals, as well as in Susana Torre, "Building Utopia: Mary Otis Stevens and the Lincoln, Massachusetts, House," in *Impossible to Hold: Women and Culture in the 1960s* (New York: NYU Press, 2005), 29–42; and Liane Lefaivre, "Living outside the Box: Mary Otis Stevens and Thomas McNulty's Lincoln House," *Harvard Design Magazine* 24 (Spring/Summer 2006): 1–5.

17. The benchmark boulder prevented Hoover from excavating the entire lower space, and he thus divided it into two separate segments.

18. Hoover thought brick for the curved fireplace wall with hearth and raised platform would make a stronger design. Brick flooring is used for all public areas except the living room.

19. A drawing exists of the furniture arrangement of the study and master bedroom, of which the Hoover family has a copy.

20. In other words, Hoover did not inform his pinwheel by applying a mathematical ratio but by studying the landscape. The authors thank Elizabeth Grossman for her observation on the "golden section" ratio found in the spiral of a nautilus shell. See n. 13, above, for Rowe's application of the word "pinwheel" to modern house plans.

21. Hoover's other fully realized residential project of virtually the same year, the Raymond and Davina Justi House, was wholly rectilinear. It was demolished sometime after 1975 by a subsequent owner. A description of the house was published, with floor plan and photographs, in "Privacy When and Where Needed," *Building Ideas* (Fall/Winter 1975): 98–100.

22. Subsequent changes in 1992 by Hartwright Partners, Inc., of Concord, Massachusetts, and in 2000 and 2006 by Boger Construction Company, of Boston, Massachusetts, did not affect the house's footprint.

23. Murphy attended Boston Architectural College between 1926 and 1930 while also working as a draftsman for various architects, among them P. A. Hopkins of Boston and B. A. Annable of Springfield, Massachusetts. In 1930 he became a Corporation Architect for H. P. Hood and Sons and a member of the American Institute of Architects in 1942. He is known to have designed at least one other residence, now demolished, in Lincoln, for himself and his wife. Persis Murphy stated in 1971 that, in addition to his forty years with Hood, her husband had "designed a few houses and one garage, gas station complex in Lincoln + the town 'barn' in Lincoln." For this information we thank John C. MacLean, the Archives of the A.I.A., and the Boston Architectural College.

24. Lincoln Building Department records do not indicate who built first, Hoover or Murphy.

25. The screen porch, whose roofline and height are informed by those of the existing structure, is remarkably airy and large. Hoover initially worried that it might seem out of proportion to the rest of the house, quipping in an undated letter to his son that it seemed like "a house attached to a porch." During the process of construction, however, both Hoover and the Gieses decided upon its present size. The porch is roofed with Visqueen, as was the original passageway.

26. In 2004, architect Gary Wolf further modified the house to accommodate the Gieses's retirement lifestyle. He enlarged the house and added exterior storage space by spinning off

two sheds beyond the carport, seemingly in random order, "like die," as Wolf put it. Overall, his design seems to reflect Hoover's own philosophy of adaptation—valuing change while respecting what was, in this case, Hoover's original scheme. The Murphy-Hoover-Wolf House was the subject of an article by Andrew Caffrey, "A Reverent Renovation," *Boston Globe Magazine* (June 10, 2007): 64–69.

27. Architect Peter Thomas was responsible for the garage's design.

28. Hoover was eighty-four years old in 1986. Anne Satterfield, in her Christmas card to Hoover of 1987, enclosed "pictures [of the causeway] for proof of <u>non</u> senility if needed in court. Afterwards maybe your children would like to see what you've been doing."

29. Bills to the Satterfields from Hoover itemize six "Landscape projects" between October and December 1987. The Satterfields sent Hoover on October 1987 a postcard of Claude Monet's water garden at Giverny containing this message: "Here's another bridge/deck/walkway for you to pursue. We saw this last June on a warm sunny day. Should we add a few vines? Yes or no. Thank you for all your great ideas. Best wishes. Anne & Chuck."

30. One other instance in Hoover's work of a gazebo-like structure was the pool-side pavilion designed for Edgar Moor on Tabor Hill Road, mentioned in Chapter 6. It "survives" in Hoover's drawing for it in O'Gorman, ed., *Drawing Toward Home*, 204–5, illustrated with detail on the back cover. This garden structure, so redolent of Hoover's work with Steele, was destroyed along with the house in 1996.

10 FINAL WORD

1. Hoover, in letter to his son, following an exhibition of Hoover's architectural work on photographic display at the Lincoln Public Library in 1979.

2. Abigail Shearer Robinson, email to authors, October 10, 2012.

3. Comment by Jean-Jacques Haffner about Hoover in 1926; see Chapter 1.

APPENDIX B

1. Statement found on sheet entitled "The Following are questions asked of the Lincoln Building Committee concerning the proposed plan for the library addition with the Committee's answers." The response quoted was to the specific question, "Will the addition be unattractive and architecturally offensive?" Lincoln Public Library Archives, Series 1, Planning, 2008–007.1.1, Box 1, folder 1, p. 2 (dated by hand 1958 on top sheet).

2. John C. MacLean and Margaret Mutchler Martin, *Lincoln Libraries 1798–1984* (Lincoln Center, MA: Lincoln Historical Society, 1984), 97. A fuller description of the library can be found in pp. 96–98.

3. Margaret Mutchler Martin, *Inheritance: Lincoln's Public Buildings in the Historic District* (Lincoln Center, MA: Lincoln Historical Society, 1987), 52. For floor plans, see p. 77.

4. A drawing exists in Hoover's hand of the "children's reading room," showing placement of furniture and shelves. Lincoln Public Library Archives, Series 8, 1958 Addition, 2003.034.8.1. Box 5 folder 99.

5. Brannan provided the date of the drawing, a copy of which is in the Lincoln Public Library Archives.

6. Information taken from MacLean and Martin, *Lincoln Libraries 1798–1984*, 97, 99. That source cites Lincoln architect Robert C. Brannan of Jung/Brannan Associates, Inc., as consultant for the 1970 renovation and architect for design of the vault.

7. MacLean and Martin, *Lincoln Libraries 1798–1984*, 96.

8. See Appendix C for particulars.

INDEX

Note: Houses discussed are in uppercase by client name.
Page numbers in *italics* refer to the illustrations.

Adams, J. Quincy, 36, 46
Adler, Bruce (client), 130n17
ADLER HOUSE, 47–51, *48*; Harold and
    Ruth Adler, 47–48; Hoover on, 48–50;
    materials, 49; projected work for, 51,
    130n17, 130n18; siting and landscape,
    48, *49*
Alofsin, Anthony, xix, 4
Anderson, Beckwith & Haible, 78, 80
Anderson, Lawrence B., 36, 78, 127n6
architects, mid-century modern,
    practicing in Lincoln, MA. *See* Adams,
    J. Quincy; Anderson, Lawrence
    B.; Bogner, Walter; Breuer, Marcel;
    Gropius, Walter; Hill, Walter L.;
    Hoover, Henry B.; Koch, Carl;
    Murphy, Cyrus; Perkins, G. Holmes;
    Pertzoff, Constantin; Stubbins, Hugh
art deco, 1, 23, 123n21
Arthur W. Wheelright Fellowship, 18
Atwood, Dorothy, 79–80, 81. *See also*
    Hoover and Hill Associates

Bauhaus, 9, 31–32
Beaux-Arts: Beaux-Arts Institute of
    Design, NYC, 1, 3, 4; École des Beaux-
    Arts, 1, 4, 7; method, xix, 1, 3, 4, 7, 12,
    17, 26. *See also* Harvard University,
    School of Architecture; University
    of Washington, Department of
    Architecture
Beaver Pond Road, 46
Behrens, Peter, 9
Black, Everett and Ann (client), 131n44

Blue Steps, 14, 16, *16*, *17*. *See also*
    Naumkeag; Steele, Fletcher
Bogner, Walter F., 36, 46, 101
Bolt, Richard and Katherine (client), 52
Breuer, Marcel, xix, 24, 36, 101
Brown's Wood, 46–47
Burnell, George, 81. *See also* industrial
    design
Buy Yourself, 84, 86, 87, *87*. *See also*
    Neumann, Ernest P.

Cambridge Reservoir, 19, 23, 28, 30,
    48–51, 52, 53, 54, 101
Cambridge School of Domestic
    Architecture and Landscape
    Architecture, 7, 33. *See also* Haffner,
    Jean-Jacques; Steele, Fletcher
Campobello, Richard and Phyllis (client),
    131n44
Cascieri, Archangelo. *See* Naumkeag
Charles Eliot Prize, 120n45
Choate, Mabel. *See* Naumkeag
Clients. *See* ADLER; Adler; Black; Bolt;
    Campobello; Cole; Crandall; Davis;
    DENORMANDIE; DeNormandie;
    Dubin; Faran; FITTS; Fleck; Flint; GER-
    MESHAUSEN; GIESE; GILBOY; HECK;
    HOOVER; Janes; Justi; Kasparian; Lee;
    Lowe; Lucas; MACLAURIN; Moor; Nel-
    son; PEAVY; RITSHER; Sandler; SAT-
    TERFIELD; SCHMERTZLER-OSBORNE;
    SHEARER; Slone; WADE; Wales;
    Wexler; Wilkoff; Witherby. *See also*
    Hoover, Henry B.: residential work

Cole, Alan and Patricia (client). *See* Fixler,
    David
Compton + Pierce, 60. *See also*
    SCHMERTZLER-OSBORNE HOUSE;
    Peacock Farm
Conant, Kenneth J., 6
Conantum, 73, 78. *See also* MACLAURIN
    HOUSE
Cornish, Joseph, 101. *See also* Historic
    New England
Cram, Ralph Adams, 9
Crandall, Stephen and Patricia (client), 52
Cret, Paul, 1, 4

Davis, Saville and Anita (client), 129n1
DENORMANDIE HOUSE, 36–39, *37*, *38*,
    40, 42, 53, 62; alteration by Hoover,
    128n6; Hoover on, 128n2; materials,
    38; Robert and Alice DeNormandie,
    36; siting, 36–37
DeNormandie, James and Martha
    (client), 39, 67
design characteristics. *See* Hoover, Henry
    B.: residential work
Dubin, Steven (client), 131n41

Edgell, George H., 1, 4–7, *8*, 9, 11, 17, 31.
    See also Harvard University, School of
    Architecture
Eugene Dodd Medal, 7

Faran, James and Ellen (client), 52
FITTS HOUSE, 39–42, *39*, *40*, *41*, 52, 53;
    another client on, 67; Charles and

Gertrude Fitts, 39, 52, 67; furnishings 42; Hoover on landscape plan, 42; materials, 42; siting, 39

Fixler, David, 64, 132n54

Fleck, James (client), 129n1

Flint, George and Lucie (client), 128n2

Fogg Art Museum, 31–32

Frederick Sheldon Fellowship, 7, 8

Friends of Modern Architecture/Lincoln, MA, 117n2, 117n6

Fulkerson, Carol J., 8, 33

Fuller, Buckminster, 31–32

furniture and furnishings. *See* FITTS HOUSE; GILBOY HOUSE; HOOVER HOUSE; SATTERFIELD HOUSE; SHEARER HOUSE

Garnier, Tony, 12

GERMESHAUSEN HOUSE, 63–67, *63, 64, 65, 66*; another client on, 66; Fixler on, 64, 132n54; homeowner on, 66; Kenneth and Polly Germeshausen, 63; materials, 66–67; siting and landscape, 63–64, 67

Giedion, Sigfried, 32

GIESE HOUSE, 95–97, *95, 96*; Hoover on, 137n25; materials, 97; Paul and Lucretia Giese, 95–96; siting, 96

GILBOY HOUSE, 27–31, *28, 29, 30, 31, 32, 37, 40, 41*; art deco detailing in, 23; furnishings, 30–31; Glennon and Elizabeth Gilboy, 27; homeowner on, 126n34; Hoover on, 28; materials, 30, 31, 125n29, 125n30, 125n32; siting, 27–28

Goldberger, Paul, 4

Goodhue, Bertram Grosvenor, 6

Gould, Carl F., 1, 3. *See also* University of Washington, Department of Architecture

Gropius, Walter, xix, 4, 6, 9, 32, 36, 46, 99, 101

Gross, Fritz, 35

Grossman, Elizabeth, 131n36, 133n62

Guévrékien, Gabriel, 12

Haffner, Jean-Jacques, 7–8, 17. *See also* Cambridge School of Domestic Architecture and Landscape Architecture; Harvard University, School of Architecture

Harbeson, John F., 3–4. *See also* Beaux-Arts

Harvard Society of Contemporary Art, 31–32

Harvard University, Graduate School of Design, 4, 18, 118n3

Harvard University, School of Architecture: Beaux-Arts method at, 1, 17, 26; Edgell, George H., 1, 4–7, 8, 9, 17; Haffner, Jean-Jacques, 7–8, 17

HECK HOUSE, 42–45, *42, 44, 45*; remodeling of Victorian house and landscape, 43–45; siting, 43; Stanley and Mary Heck, 42–43; threatened with demolition, xix, 62, 95

Hill, Walter Lee, 46, 78–80. *See also* Hoover and Hill Associates

Historic New England, 26, 101, 125n25

Hitchcock, Henry-Russell, 11, 31–32

Hood, Raymond, 6

Hoover, Henry B.
—biography: birth and death, xix, xx, 1, 97; civic positions in Lincoln, MA, 36; discovery of Lincoln, 18; teaching (*see* Lowthorpe School of Landscape Architecture for Women); travel letters from Europe 8–11, 18
—education, graduate, xix, 4–7; degree 4, 11; fellowships and prizes, 7, 8, 120n45
—education, undergraduate, xix, 1, 3; degree 1; mentions 4, 119n19
—family life: Elizabeth (daughter), Henry B., Jr. (son), and Lucretia (daughter), 18, 23, 35; Lucretia Jones (wife), 80, 81, 123n18, 135n21
—residential work: affiliated with Harvard University, 67, 130n21, 130n25; affiliated with M.I.T., 27, 57, 63, 73, 89, 130n21, 130n25; for clients not named by house, 39, 48, 52, 67, 79, 128n2, 129n1, 130n17, 131n44, 132n45, 132n48, 137n21; comments from clients, 53, 57, 58, 61, 62, 63, 66, 73, 75, 79, 94, 97,

99, 132n50, 137n9; comments from subsequent homeowners, xx, 58, 66, 126n34, 131n34; comments on own work, 19, 26, 28, 32, 43, 48, 49–50, 62, 77, 79, 91, 99, 128n2, 130n13, 130n17, 130n18; delayed entry, 21, 24, 26, 28, 30, 31, 37–38, 40, 49, 54, 58, 68; design characteristics, summarized, 17, 21, 46; hexagonal plan, *xxi, 47*; H-plan, 49, 60, 61, 68, 75; integration of architecture and landscape, 21, 28, 31, 39, 42, 44, 48, 49–50, 53, 54, 58, 61, 62, 63–64, 67, 70, 73, 75, 77, 89, 92, 94–95, 96, 97; modern materials and technology, 5, 23, 26, 42, 51, 55, 77, 124n14, 124n16, 125n22, 137n25; modular plan, 58, 61, 70, 75, 77; partnership (*see* Hoover and Hill Associates); sectional scheme, 23, 28, 30, 53, 58, 61, 63–64, 68, 75; shaping of volumes, 23, 30, 40–41, 49, 58, 68, 77, 90; siting, 21, 27–28, 39, 48, 50, 53, 57, 63–64, 66, 67, 70, 73, 75, 92; splayed plan, 28, 31, 32, 37, 53, 54; symmetrical plan, 43, 64, 66, 77, 90; use of atrium, 61, 77. *See also individual clients by house*
—nonresidential work: Fletcher Steele, association with, xix, 8, 11, 12, 13–14, 17, 18, 19, 33, 40, 99, 121n66, 121n68, 122n9 (*see also* Naumkeag); industrial design, 33, 46, 81–87, 99 (*see also* Buy Yourself); parsonage, First Parish, Lincoln, 111; public buildings, 131n40 (*see also* Lincoln Public Library (addition); Lincoln Public School Buildings); World War II, 32, 33, 36 (*see also* Raytheon Manufacturing Company)

Hoover, Lucretia Jones, 80, 135n21

Hoover and Hill Associates: Hill comment on, 79; office configuration, 79–80, 135n21; office personnel (*see* Atwood, Dorothy; Miller, John; Wood, Joan); office projects, 80, 81, 83–84, 87; partnership, 46, 78–80, 89

HOOVER HOUSE, 8–28, *21, 22, 23, 24, 25, 98*; alteration by Hoover, 24, 26, *26, 27*, 101; art deco detailing in, 23; conceptual drawing, 18–19,

19; furnishings, 23–24; Henry and Lucretia Hoover, 18–19; Hoover on, 19, 26; landscape, 19, 20; materials, 21, 23, 26, 124n14, 124n16, 125n22; siting, 19. *See also* Historic New England

Hoover houses, plans, 24, 26, 28, 38, 39, 44, 49, 55, 60, 61, 64, 70, 75, 90, 93, 96

Hoover houses, principal locations, 109–15

Howe & Lescaze, 6

Huckleberry Hill Road, 46–48, 51, 129n8

Hudnut, Joseph F., 18, 118n3. *See also* Gropius, Walter; Harvard University, Graduate School of Design

Hurd, Christopher, 52. *See also* Tabor Hill Road

industrial design, 33, 46, 81–87, 82, 83, 85, 86, 87, 99. *See also* Hoover, Henry B.: nonresidential work

international style, 11, 31. *See also* Hitchcock, Henry-Russell; Johnson, Philip

Janes, Sargent and Ann (client), 132n48

Johnson, Philip, 11, 31–32

Justi, Raymond and Davina (client), 132n48, 136n7, 137n21

Karson, Robin, 11, 13, 17

Kasparian, Karl and Carol (client), 48, 129n10

Kendrick, John S., 81

Kimball, S. Fiske, 5–6

Koch, Carl, 36, 73, 78, 101. *See also* Conantum

Korean War, 67, 78. *See also* Hoover and Hill Associates

Le Corbusier, 6, 9, 12

Lee, Edgar and Florence (client), 132n48, 136n17

Lincoln, MA: development of, 36, 46; discovery by Hoover, 18

Lincoln Public Library (addition), 46, 80, 105–7, 106

Lincoln Public School buildings, 46, 78, 80

Lowe, E. M. (client), 32, 92

Lowthorpe School of Landscape Architecture for Women, 33–34, 34, 35. *See also* Steele, Fletcher

Lucas, Homer and Lela (client), 131n44

Lurçat, André, 12

MACLAURIN HOUSE, 73–77, 74, 75, 76; client and homeowner on, 75; Elfriede Maclaurin, 73, 75; Hoover on, 77; materials, 77; siting, 75

Manning, Warren H., 7. *See also* Steele, Fletcher

Massachusetts Institute of Technology, architect graduates. *See* Anderson, Lawrence B., Compton + Pierce; Hill, Walter Lee

materials, modern. *See* Hoover, Henry B.: residential work

Mendelsohn, Erich, 9

Mies van der Rohe, Ludwig, 9

Miller, John, 81. *See also* Hoover and Hill Associates

modernism in New England, xx, 4, 6, 32, 36, 46, 99, 126n38, 126n39

Moor, Edgar (client), 51–52; house, 52; pavilion, 53, 54

Murphy, Cyrus, 96, 125n24, 137n23

Museum of Modern Art, 31–32

Naumkeag, 12–13, 13, 14, 16, 16, 17. *See also* Blue Steps; Steele, Fletcher

Nelson, Arthur H. and Eleanor (client), 75; client, Hoover, Hill on house, 79

Nelson Robinson Fellowship, 8

Neumann, Ernest P., 84, 87

Neutra, Richard, 24

Ochsner, Jeffrey, 118n7

Old Concord Road, 46, 75

Olmsted, Frederick Law, Jr., 7

Oud, J. J. P., 6, 9

Paine Furniture Company, 39, 67, 132n60. *See also* FITTS HOUSE; SHEARER HOUSE

Peacock Farm, *xx*, 60

Pearmain, Robert, 51, 57. *See also* Tabor Hill Road

PEAVY HOUSE, 52–57, 55, 56, 57, 79; client on, 53; furnishings, 53, 130n28; Leo and Elizabeth Peavy, 52, 75; materials, 55, 130n29; siting, 53

Perkins, G. Holmes, 36

Pertzoff, Constantin, 36, 46–47

Raymond, Eleanor, 11

Raytheon Manufacturing Company, 33; Hoover design work for, 34–35, 47, 81, 84

RITSHER HOUSE, 91–95, 92, 93, 94; client on, 94, 137n9; furnishings, 137n19; Hoover on, 91; John and Cynthia Ritsher, 91; materials, 137n18; siting, 91

Sandler, Allan and Mary (client), 131n41, 132n45

SATTERFIELD CAUSEWAY, 97; client on, 97, 138n28, 138n29

SATTERFIELD HOUSE, 52, 57–58, 59, 60, 61; Charles and Anne Satterfield, 57–58; client on, 57, 58; furnishings, 58; homeowner on, 58, 131n34; materials, 58, 131n35; siting, 57–58

SCHMERTZLER-OSBORNE HOUSE, 58–63, 61, 62; additions by Hoover for Louis and Barbara Osborne, 61–62, 132n47; Alvin and Barbara Schmertzler, 58, 60; client on, 61, 62–63, 132n50; Hoover on, 62; materials, 62, 132n48; siting, 60, 62

Scott, Giles Gilbert, 9

Sert, José Luis, 78

SHEARER HOUSE, 67–73, 68, 69, 70, 72, 73, 95; client on, 73; daughter on, 99; furnishings, 68, 71, 125n33, 132n60; materials, 68; rediscovery of, 132n56; siting, 67, 70; William and Constance Shearer, 67. *See also* Paine Furniture Company

Shurcliff, Arthur, 7

siting. *See* Hoover, Henry B.: residential

work; *and individual clients by name and by house*

Slone, Dennis and Anetta (client), 131n41, 131n44

Steele, Fletcher: as author, 12, 17; association with Haffner, 7; association with Hoover, xix, 8, 11, 12, 13–14, 17, 18, 19, 33, 40, 99, 121n66, 121n68, 122n9; association with Lowthorpe School, 33; awareness of modernism, 12, 31, 123n21; education and creation of firm, 7–8

Stevens-McNulty House, 92

Stratford Realty Company, Inc., 47; Stratford Way, Lincoln, MA, 51, 130n17, 130n18. *See also* Adler House

Stubbins, Hugh, 36

subdivisions, mid-century modern, in Lincoln, Lexington, and Concord, 46–47, 51, 52, 60, 73, 78. *See also* Beaver Pond Road, Brown's Wood, Conantum, Huckleberry Hill Road, Old Concord Road, Peacock Farm, Tabor Hill Road, Twin Pond Lane, Woodcock Lane, Woods End Road

Sullivan, Louis, 6

Tabor Hill Road, 6, 46–47, 51, 52, 57

Twin Pond Lane, 46–47

University of Washington, Department of Architecture: Beaux-Arts Institute of Design program, NYC, 1, 4; Beaux-Arts method at, xix, 1, 17, 26; Gould, Carl F., 1, 3; program of study, 1, 3

WADE HOUSE, 88–91, 88, 90; client on Hoover, 90–91; Jeptha and Emily Wade, 89; materials, 89; siting, 89

Wales, Langdon and Ruth (client), 132n48, 134n20

Weatherhead, Arthur C., 3–4. *See also* Beaux-Arts

Wexler, Robert and Shirley (client), 129n1

Wilkoff, Howard and Ida (client), *xxi*, 47, 129n1

Witherby, Thomas and Marianne (client), 48, 129n1, 129n10

Wolf, Gary, 122n70

Wood, Joan, 79, 81, 123n26. *See also* Hoover and Hill Associates

Woodcock Lane, 46–47

Woods End Road, 46, 101

World War II, 32, 33–35, 36. *See also* Lowthorpe School of Landscape Architecture for Women; Raytheon Manufacturing Company

Wright, Frank Lloyd, 6–7, 32, 53